dare to dream!
25 extraordinary lives

"Every young person needs a hero. All kids need someone who will stand by them, coach them when they have a tough decision to make, help them keep their priorities in order, hold them accountable for their words and actions, and generally be their number-one cheerleader. *Dare to Dream!* does just this. It gives our young people *real* heroes they can respect and emulate."

> —*Terry Hitchcock, PhD,*
> *Executive Director, the Heroes & Dreams Foundation*

"*Dare to Dream!* will encourage children to set goals and then work hard to overcome the obstacles which might prevent them from achieving those goals."

> —*Daniel R. Hart,*
> *Retired Hennepin County, Minnesota, District Court Judge*

"Every youth, regardless of background, needs one thing: hope. *Dare to Dream!* conveys through real-life stories of well-known, accomplished people from all walks of life and every form of diversity that even humps and bumps, deep valleys, and wide rivers on life's road need not diminish dreams or delimit destiny. . . . The author succeeds marvelously through story form in helping to make hope become a reality in the lives of our youth today."

> —*Donald Draayer, PhD,*
> *National Superintendent of the Year, 1990, and teacher,*
> *administrator, and educational consult for 46 years*

"In *Dare to Dream!* you will find stories of individuals from all walks of life who've become heroes because they held firmly to their beliefs and worked hard to realize their dreams. We encourage every young reader of this book to do both. By believing in yourself and reaching for the stars, not only will you achieve your goals, you will become exactly who you want to be—someone who deserves and receives the respect of family, friends, and peers."

> —*Sara O'Meara, Chairman and CEO, and*
> *Yvonne Fedderson, President,*
> *Childhelp USA*

"*Dare to Dream!* is the kind of book for young people that I 'dare to dream' about. Instead of emphasizing just sports and entertainment and lifestyles of the rich and famous as so much of the media does, it talks about the choices and hard work that were involved in creating success in the lives of many well-known individuals who faced substantial obstacles. . . . I hope it will become a staple in middle schools throughout the country."

> —*Benjamin S. Carson Sr., MD,*
> *Professor and Director of Pediatric Neurosurgery,*
> *Johns Hopkins School of Medicine*

dare to dream!
25 extraordinary lives

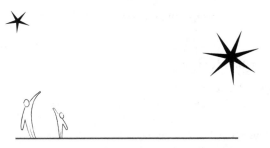

Sandra McLeod Humphrey

Prometheus Books

59 John Glenn Drive
Amherst, New York 14228-2119

Published 2005 by Prometheus Books

Inquiries should be addressed to
Prometheus Books
59 John Glenn Drive
Amherst, New York 14228–2119
VOICE: 716–691–0133, ext. 210
FAX: 716–691–0137
WWW.PROMETHEUSBOOKS.COM

14 13   11

Library of Congress Cataloging-in-Publication Data

Humphrey, Sandra McLeod.
   Dare to dream! : 25 extraordinary lives / Sandra McLeod Humphrey.
      p. cm.
   Includes bibliographical references.
   ISBN 978–1–59102–280–0 (alk. paper)
   1. Heroes—United States—Biography. 2. Successful people—United States—Biography. 3. Achievement motivation—United States. 4. Achievement motivation in youth—United States. 5. Courage. I. Title.

CT215.H86 2005
920.73—dc22

                                                    2004027190

Printed in the United States of America on acid-free paper

Heroes are ordinary people who accomplish
extraordinary things, and this book is dedicated
to all our heroes—past, present, and future.

The greater danger for most of us
is not that our aim is too high
and we miss it,
but that it is too low
and we reach it.

—Michelangelo
(1475–1564)

table of **contents**

Contents

a note **to adults**

Many of our young people today are lacking heroes, goals, and a sense of direction to their lives.

The intent of this book is to restore dreams and heroes to our young people—not magical heroes with no problems but real heroes who have had a dream, have committed themselves to that dream, and have then worked hard and overcome obstacles to attain that dream.

This book is therefore dedicated to young people everywhere to encourage them to have a dream and then commit themselves to that dream and never give up.

a note to the young reader

As you read the following biographical sketches, you will see that no one individual excelled at everything but that each had his own unique gifts and talents. You will also notice that there are certain similarities which occur consistently and repeatedly throughout the biographies.

They all had courage. Some had physical courage, some had moral courage, and some had spiritual courage, but they all were willing to take risks and stand by their convictions even when sometimes it meant standing alone.

They all made a personal commitment to a dream and then had the patience, perseverance, and determination to pursue that dream in spite of frustrations and discouragement. They were marathon runners rather than sprinters, and they hung in there for the entire race.

They all had obstacles to overcome. Some were physical obstacles (such as a physical handicap, a lack of athletic ability, or a lack of physical beauty), some were psychological obstacles (such as extreme shyness or feelings of inferiority), some were financial obstacles (such as the expectations and responsibilities associated with great wealth or the burdens of extreme poverty), and some were social obstacles (such as racial discrimination or educational deprivation). Some rose above their obstacles by working hard and believing in themselves, and some turned their apparent disadvantage to advantage by a change in their own attitude.

And lastly, all had a larger perspective than self. Their fulfillment came not from personal recognition or materialistic success but rather from their dedication to improving the lives of those around them.

Abraham **Lincoln**

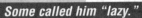
Some called him "lazy."

AP Photo/Alexander Gardner

As a boy:

He was born in a one-room log cabin in Kentucky, one of the slave states, in 1809, and named Abraham after his grandfather.

When he was seven years old, his family moved to Indiana, which was a free state where no slavery was allowed.

In Indiana he and his older sister Sally hiked nine miles each way to school through timberland where bear, deer, coon, and wildcats ran wild.

His father felt it was a waste of time to send his children to school nine miles away just to sit with a lot of other children and learn all day, but his mother Nancy encouraged his schooling and told him to learn all he could.

His mother Nancy died when he was nine, and their home became dreary and cheerless until his father remarried a year later. Abraham sometimes said that his stepmother Sarah was the best friend he ever had, and he called her his "angel mother."

He was always asking questions that irritated his father, and many nights he lay awake thinking about long words like "independent" and "predestination."

As he grew older, he was not considered to be particularly attractive physically, and some considered him homely. He was described as gangly, awkward, and "appearing to be all joints."

He moved slowly and awkwardly, tended to walk with a slouch, and was so tall that he had to duck his head to go through a door.

He was different from his friends in that he didn't like to play cards, drink, or hunt. He shot a prairie turkey when he was eleven and never shot any game again after that.

His friends and some of his relatives thought he was "peculiarsome" because he spent so much time reading books, and he was known to walk as far as twenty miles just to borrow a book.

His stepmother Sarah encouraged him to read and study, but his father thought his son's interest in books and education was a sign of laziness.

Even though his father thought books were a "waste of time," Abraham loved books more than anything else and read all the books available within a fifty-mile radius of his home.

He always told people that he learned slowly but that his mind was like a piece of metal because it was "hard to scratch anything on it and impossible to get it off after it was on."

A neighbor he worked for complained that he was "always reading and thinking" and considered him "awful lazy."

He never had any real companionship with his father, but he had a deep affection for his stepmother, who understood his need to learn and encouraged him to read as much as he could.

Although he had very little formal education (less than one year altogether), he had an unquenchable thirst for learning. He always said the things he wanted to know were in books and that his best friend was "the man who'll git me a book I ain't read."

Even though he was the best runner, jumper, and wrestler in several counties, his first love was always books and learning.

As a man:

At age nineteen, he left his family in Illinois and worked as a helper on a flatboat down the Mississippi River to New Orleans, where he saw a slave auction.

When he saw how black people were treated like property in the South, it made a lasting impression on him. He vowed to fight against slavery in any way he could.

When he was twenty-two, he returned to Illinois to work as a clerk in a store, but the store failed. He then tried running a store of his own, but his store also failed, and it took him many years to pay off all his debts.

Besides being a river boatman and a storekeeper, he also was a rail splitter, a postmaster, a surveyor, a captain in the militia, and he taught himself law.

When he was twenty-three, he campaigned for a seat in the Illinois legislature but was defeated. He ran again two years later, and this time he was elected and served from 1834 to 1841.

People said that as a lawyer, he was popular but not gifted, and as a politician, he was gifted but not always popular.

He was elected to the US House of Representatives in 1846 and served one term. Then in 1860 he was elected the sixteenth president of the United States.

After his election, seven southern states seceded from the Union and formed their own government. They called themselves

15

the Confederate States of America, and they even elected their own president, Jefferson Davis. The country was now divided!

When Confederate guns fired on Fort Sumter on April 12, 1861, the Civil War began, and there were now eleven states in the Confederacy—all slave states.

Slavery had caused the war, and he knew there could be no peace if the country remained half-slave and half-free. So in 1863 he signed the Emancipation Proclamation, which declared all slaves in the rebelling southern states to be free. He considered this the most important act of his entire administration.

He was also a gifted writer and orator, and his Gettysburg Address (1863) is still considered one of the greatest speeches delivered by anyone at any time in history.

Without his wise and firm leadership during the Civil War, our country might have remained divided into two separate nations. He embodied the spirit of freedom and democracy and proved to the whole world that "government of the people, by the people, and for the people" would not perish from the earth.

He was reelected president of the United States in 1864, but he was shot by John Wilkes Booth, a deranged actor, on April 14, 1865—just five days after General Lee's surrender at Appomattox, Virginia, which marked the end of the Civil War.

He is still considered to be one of our greatest presidents, and although he died over one hundred years ago, his leadership and courage still serve as examples to people everywhere.

"A house divided against itself cannot stand."
—Abraham Lincoln (1809–1865)

Thomas Alva **Edison**

AP Photo

As a boy:

He was born in 1847 in Milan, Ohio, and even as a young boy, his curiosity was always getting him into trouble.

He always wanted to know "why." At age three he fell into a grain elevator and almost drowned in the grain because he wanted to see how the elevator worked. And at age four, his father found him squatting on some duck eggs in a cold barn to see if he could hatch the eggs instead of the mother duck.

He had very little formal education because his teachers thought his constant questions were a sign of stupidity. So, when he was seven, his mother, who had been a teacher, took him out of school and taught him at home.

17

Dare to Dream!

Some of the neighbors thought this strange child with the small body and unusually large head who asked so many questions must be "addled," and even the local doctor feared that he might have "brain trouble" because of his very large head.

He loved to read and chemistry books were his favorite books, but he did more than just read them. He tried many of the experiments the books described to prove to himself that the facts in the books were really true.

When he was about ten, he set up a chemistry lab in the basement in his home, and during one of his experiments, he set the basement on fire and nearly blew himself up.

Then when he was twelve, in order to earn money to pay for the chemicals for his experiments, he went into business selling candy and newspapers on the local train and worked on his scientific experiments in his spare time.

He was forced to stop his experiments temporarily when a stick of phosphorus started a fire in the crude lab he had set up in the baggage car. The conductor threw him and all his equipment off the train at the next stop.

It seemed he was always experimenting. Once he gave a friend a triple dose of seidlitz powders, hoping that enough gas would be generated to enable him to fly. This resulted in terrible agonies for his friend and a whipping for him.

At sixteen he was given the chance to learn how to be a telegraph operator, and he then became as fascinated by electricity as he had been by chemistry.

Unfortunately, he was a very undependable telegraph operator because his mind was usually more on the ideas in his head than on the work he was supposed to be doing.

During his first year as a telegrapher, he was fired from four jobs because he spent so much of his time reading books, performing experiments, or catching up on his sleep.

In telegraphy circles he became known as "The Looney" because he spent so much of his time reading and experimenting.

The other telegraph operators laughed at him and made jokes about his shabby clothes and shaggy hair. And his employers were often impatient with him, considering him to be "an impractical, dreamy young fellow who would probably never amount to much."

As a man:

By age twenty-one, he had changed from experimenter to inventor and had decided to work on his inventions full time. He had so many ideas for inventions that he knew he would have to work very hard to do everything he wanted to do.

As the market for his inventions grew, he found he needed a larger facility. So in 1876 he moved to Menlo Park, New Jersey, where he established his own research center. There he gathered together the best craftsmen and scientists he could find and put them to work in what he called his "idea factory."

A year later he introduced his first great invention, the phonograph, to the world. With his invention of the phonograph, he became a celebrity, but this was just the beginning.

In 1879, after many months of hard work, he demonstrated his greatest invention—the electric lightbulb—which changed the way people lived forever.

All through his life he asked questions and wanted to know "why." Then he proceeded to figure out a new and better way of doing things.

He had infinite patience and seldom became discouraged. He tackled every problem with a positive attitude and never gave up until he had solved it. He frequently worked eighteen hours a day, and during his life, he was granted more than a thousand separate patents for his inventions.

It is because of his natural curiosity and belief in hard work that our world today is a much better place in which to live.

No other man has done so much to apply scientific discovery to everyday life as he did with his inventions of the phonograph (which he considered his greatest invention), the electric lightbulb, the typewriter, the dictating machine, the electric dynamo, the motion picture camera, and many others. He also improved such inventions as the telephone and the telegraph.

Never discouraged by what other people called his "failures," he saw them as necessary steps in the scientific process.

He made and directed the first silent movie and invented the "talking picture" by combining two of his greatest inventions: the phonograph and the motion picture camera. Through his inventions of the phonograph and the motion picture camera, he has probably done more to entertain the world than any other man.

Although he became a multimillionaire, he remained modest and was always happiest when in his lab working on a new invention.

He was awarded the Congressional Medal of Honor in 1928, and on the day he died, at age eighty-four, President Herbert Hoover asked everyone in America to turn off their electric lights for one hour in tribute to the inventive genius of this man.

He was one of the greatest inventors the world has ever known and more than attained his goal of trying to improve the well-being of the common man. He has provably brought more comfort and pleasure into our daily lives than any other inventor in history.

"Genius is 1 percent inspiration and 99 percent perspiration."
—Thomas Alva Edison (1847–1931)

Nellie **Bly**

She called herself a "lonely orphan girl."

As a girl:

Elizabeth Jane Cochran was born in 1864 in Cochran's Mills, Pennsylvania, a town named after its most prominent citizen, her father.

Her father, Michael Cochran, was a man of great determination and ambition who had made his own way in the world—from a simple blacksmith to a prosperous and influential landowner and judge.

Very likely Elizabeth inherited her determination and strong will from her father and her dramatic flare from her mother.

Elizabeth was christened in a bright pink gown, and while other little girls were dressed in drab browns and grays, Elizabeth's mother dressed her in frilly pink frocks.

Pink was always Elizabeth's favorite color, and she wore pink so often that she was given the nickname Pink.

Her father encouraged her to read books, and from the very beginning, she loved to read and write stories.

But when Elizabeth was six, her life changed dramatically. Her father died after being struck suddenly with a paralyzing illness.

Although he had been a prominent member of the community, he died without leaving a will. With no legal claim to his property, Elizabeth's mother was forced to auction off his estate, and the family was forced to move to a much smaller home.

Hoping to provide for her five children financially, Elizabeth's mother married again. Unfortunately, Elizabeth's stepfather was physically abusive and, at age fourteen, Elizabeth had to testify in court to help her mother obtain a divorce.

After the divorce, Elizabeth and her family moved to the noisy, smoke-blackened city of Pittsburgh, where they hoped it would be easier to find work.

During those miserable years of her mother's second marriage, Elizabeth had come to realize that she never wanted to depend on anyone but herself, and so when other young girls were choosing marriage, she chose a career instead.

But finding a job was not easy. Her brothers quickly found good white-collar jobs, but the only jobs available to girls at that time were in factories and sweatshops.

For four years she was one of the many women unable to find steady and decent-paying employment.

Then in January 1885 she read an article in the *Pittsburgh Dispatch* called "What Girls Are Good For." The article was written by Erasmus Wilson, Pittsburgh's most popular columnist, and he claimed in his article that any woman who had a job was "a monstrosity" and that women belonged in the home doing domestic tasks and raising children.

Elizabeth was so enraged by the article that she fired off an anonymous letter of protest to George Madden, managing editor of the *Dispatch*, describing the plight of the many young women who had to work to survive in industrial Pittsburgh.

That article changed her life forever!

As a woman:

George Madden was so impressed by the letter, signed "Lonely Orphan Girl," that he placed an ad in the Sunday paper asking that she introduce herself.

The following day, Elizabeth landed her first job as a journalist. And along with the job came a new name because in those days it was quite improper for a woman to write for a newspaper and make her identity known to the public.

After several suggestions from the newsroom workers, Madden chose Nellie Bly, the title character in the song "Nelly Bly" written thirty-five years earlier by Stephen Foster.

Nellie focused her attention on social injustices and was the inventor of investigative reporting. She also became an expert at undercover work, posing as a poor sweatshop worker in order to expose the cruelty and dire conditions under which women toiled.

When factory owners threatened to pull their advertising from the *Dispatch* because of her articles, Nellie persuaded her editor to send her to Mexico. While there, she wrote articles about the poverty and political corruption in Mexico, which eventually got her ejected from Mexico by the Mexican government.

Instead of returning to Pittsburgh, she went instead to New York City, hoping to find work with one of the larger newspapers. But four months later, she was still jobless and penniless.

Finally, she managed to talk her way into the offices of New York's biggest paper, the *New York World*. She was in the right place at the right time because the paper needed an undercover reporter clever enough and courageous enough to get herself committed to the Women's Lunatic Asylum at Blackwell's Island in order check out the rumors of mistreatment and abuse.

She later described the asylum as "a human rat-trap," and this adventurous and daring stunt not only propelled her into the limelight of New York journalism but also resulted in improved conditions in New York's asylums.

In the fall of 1888, when she found out the *World*'s executives were planning to send a man around the world in less than eighty days, she threatened to do it in less time for another newspaper if they did not agree to send her instead.

The trip made her an instant celebrity as the *World* published daily accounts of her travel experiences. When she completed her trip in a record-breaking seventy-two days, there was a great celebration, and a huge crowd turned out to welcome her home.

Throughout her professional life she always tried to right wrongs. From having herself committed to an insane asylum to reveal the inhumane conditions there to becoming one of the first newspaper correspondents to report from the front lines of World War I, she fought to expose injustice and corruption and helped redefine a woman's role in turn-of-the-century America.

When she died in 1922 from pneumonia, all the newspapers in New York acknowledged her passing with elaborate obituaries.

"Energy rightly applied ... will accomplish anything."
—Nellie Bly (1864–1922)

Some thought he was "backward."

AP Photo

As a boy:

Albert was born in 1879 in Ulm, Germany, and he was so slow to learn to speak that his parents thought he might be mildly retarded.

Although his family was Jewish, he attended a Catholic elementary school, where he did not excel. His teachers considered him a "misfit" because he asked so many questions, and his slow speech and shyness also made the other kids in school think he was "slow."

There is a family story that the headmaster of his school told Albert's family that it didn't matter what profession the boy prepared for because he would never be successful at anything.

He was always shy and dreamy and didn't feel comfortable with the other boys, so he spent a lot of his time alone or sitting for hours listening to his mother play the piano.

While his schoolmates were busy at boisterous games on the playground, he would stand apart, thinking his own thoughts and daydreaming. His idea of fun was to compose little songs and hymns on the family piano and then hum them to himself later when he didn't have a piano.

Many of his teachers during his early school years considered him "dull." He found languages very difficult, and since he didn't like to memorize, he did not study as much as he should have and did rather poorly in school.

At the age of twelve, he became fascinated with an algebra textbook, which he later said changed his entire life because the book opened his eyes to what man could accomplish through the "the force of thought alone."

After that, he began to read a great deal and taught himself differential and integral calculus. But he still disliked school, and at the age of fifteen, he was asked to leave his high school because his indifference to schoolwork "set a bad example" for the other students.

After he left school, he joined his family in Italy and renounced his German citizenship. He then belonged to no country until he became a Swiss citizen in 1901.

He failed the entrance exam the first time he took it for admission to the Swiss Federal Institute of Technology in Zurich, Switzerland. He did brilliantly in math and physics but failed dismally in biology, chemistry, and French.

When he was finally accepted by the Swiss Federal Institute of Technology, his academic record was never brilliant because he spent most of his time and energy on his own studies rather than on the studies assigned by the institute. He didn't care for such organized education, and he hated having to attend classes regularly and take exams.

This independent spirit later cost him a much-needed job at the institute after graduation, and he was the only one in his graduating class who was not offered an appointment as an assistant professor at the institute.

As a man:

After his graduation in 1900, he had difficulty finding a job, so he took temporary teaching jobs. Then in 1902 he got a job with the Swiss patent office, where he found time to pursue his own interests in physics and higher mathematics.

In 1905 he laid the groundwork for the atomic age by developing the formula $E = mc^2$ (energy = mass times the speed of light squared), which became probably the most famous formula in science.

What he called his special theory of relativity was considered by other scientists to be one of the most significant pieces of scientific work ever done. He had shown for the first time that there was a relationship between matter and energy and that one could be converted into the other.

He became world famous for his special theory of relativity in 1905 and for his general theory of relativity in 1916, which became the basis of modern nuclear development.

He was awarded the Nobel Prize for Physics in 1921, and he was awarded the Gold Medal of the Royal Astronomical Society in 1926. The five major research papers that he published had forever changed mankind's view of the universe.

As a Jew, he spoke out against Nazi crimes against the Jews and thus became very unpopular with the Nazis in Germany. After the Nazis came to power in Germany in 1932 and seized his property, he never returned to Germany.

He was welcomed at the Institute for Advanced Study at Princeton University, where he attempted to unify the laws of physics, and in 1940 he became an American citizen while still retaining his Swiss citizenship.

His work led indirectly to the development of the atomic bomb, which saddened him since he had not intended his work to be used for destructive purposes.

He spent his latter years campaigning for the control of nuclear weapons and for the peaceful use of atomic energy. Then in 1945 he was appointed chairman of the Emergency Committee of Atomic Scientists dedicated to furthering world peace.

In 1952 the young nation of Israel offered him the presidency, but, even though he felt very honored, he declined.

One week before his death he signed a letter to the great philosopher Bertrand Russell in which he agreed that his name should go on a manifesto urging all nations to give up nuclear weapons. It is fitting that one of his last acts was to argue, as he had done all his life, for international peace.

He was one of the greatest scientists of all time and ranks with Galileo and Isaac Newton as one who revolutionized man's concepts of space, time, matter, energy, and light and gave man a new and much more profound interest in his universe.

He was truly a concerned citizen of the entire world and one of the legendary figures of the twentieth century.

"The most incomprehensible thing about the world is that it is at all comprehensible."

—Albert Einstein (1879–1955)

Helen **Keller**

Some called her "simpleminded."

As a girl:

She was born in 1880, the daughter of a newspaper publisher, and was a very lively, healthy, and friendly child.

Then at nineteen months of age, she developed a high fever that left her deaf and blind for the rest of her life. After that, everything in her life changed dramatically.

The more frustrated she became at being unable to express herself, the more bad-tempered, angry, and unmanageable she became. She began throwing wild and unruly temper tantrums.

Her table manners were atrocious. She frequently ate with her hands rather than with a fork or spoon, and she grabbed food from other people's plates while they were still eating.

She was sullen and disheveled and often refused to even let anyone comb her hair or straighten her clothing.

Much of the time she was more like a savage animal than a human being. She screamed, she kicked, and she even bit when she was frustrated or frightened.

She tyrannized the household with her behavior: she locked people in their rooms and then hid the keys, she yanked tablecloths filled with dishes to the floor, and she scared people with her violent temper tantrums when she didn't get her own way.

Some people considered her "feebleminded," and even some of her mother's relatives thought she was mentally defective and should be "put away" in a mental institution because she was "too odd to have around and the sight of her made everyone unhappy."

It became clear that something had to be done, so just before Helen's seventh birthday, the family hired a private tutor named Anne Sullivan.

Anne was twenty-one years old and had graduated at the top of her class from the Perkins School for the Blind in Boston. She had been almost blind herself, but doctors were able to restore much of her sight. Now she wanted to help other blind children.

Having been almost blind herself, she understood Helen's frustration and anger and knew that she had to teach her how to communicate. But before she could teach this wild child, she had to control her. She finally won these difficult battles with Helen by sheer willpower and persistence.

In the beginning Helen scratched, punched, bit, and kicked Anne and even overturned furniture when Anne tried to set limits for her. During one of Helen's violent temper tantrums, she even broke two of Anne's teeth.

A real breakthrough came when Anne decided to teach her the manual alphabet—a sign language in which each letter is signed onto the hand of the deaf-blind person so that he or she can feel it.

Once Helen discovered language, she "talked" constantly. Now she could finally communicate her thoughts to others and put an end to the isolation that had kept her a prisoner for so long.

There was no stopping her now, and she studied very hard. She was determined to make up for all the time she had wasted.

As a woman:

In the fall of 1889, Helen enrolled at the Perkins Institution for the Blind. And in March 1890 she began speech lessons with Sarah Fuller, principal of the Horace Mann School for the Deaf.

Anne continued to be her constant companion, and when Helen was fourteen, she was felt to be ready for the next step in her education. She was enrolled at the Wright-Humason School in New York City, which specialized in teaching the deaf to talk.

Helen had phenomenal powers of concentration and memory as well as a dogged determination to succeed, and with Anne's help, she proved to be a remarkable scholar.

In 1904 she graduated with honors from Radcliffe College. She had accomplished the unimaginable. Blind and deaf, she had succeeded at one of the most famous schools in America!

While still in college, she wrote *The Story of My Life*, which was an immediate success and earned her enough money to buy a house for Anne and herself.

By age twenty-four, she had become world famous, but she was determined to do something with her life that would help others.

As she began to realize some of the injustices in the world, she became a suffragette, demanding equal rights for women and better pay for working-class people.

She even took more speech lessons so that she could make public speeches about the issues that concerned her.

Then she and Anne toured the country giving lectures— Anne talking about her teaching methods and Helen giving brief inspirational messages and answering questions.

As she became increasingly more famous, many books were written about her and films were made of her life.

In 1921 the American Foundation for the Blind was created, and Helen and Anne toured the country in a series of speaking engagements to raise funds for the organization.

In 1931 Helen helped organize the World Conference on Work for the Blind and persuaded President Herbert Hoover and his wife to give a reception for the conference.

Her deep need to communicate made her reach out to people, both famous and unknown. During World War II she made a cross-country tour of army hospitals, visiting the wounded soldiers, especially those who had been blinded. She later described this as "the crowning experience of my life."

She died in 1968, but she is still remembered as the woman with the remarkable spirit who overcame adversity and learned, in spite of her multiple handicaps, to communicate not only with her family and friends but with the entire world.

With the help of her teacher Anne Sullivan, and because of her own indomitable spirit, she became an author, a world traveler, and a tireless leader in the fight to improve the lives of blind and deaf people all over the world.

"Keep your face to the sunshine and you cannot see the shadows."
—Helen Keller (1880–1968)

Eleanor **Roosevelt**

Some people called her an "ugly duckling."

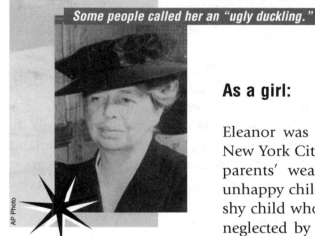

AP Photo

As a girl:

Eleanor was born in 1884 in New York City, and despite her parents' wealth, she had an unhappy childhood. She was a shy child who felt rejected and neglected by her mother, who was embarrassed by her daughter's lack of beauty and homely features. Her mother called her "Granny" even in front of visitors, which made Eleanor feel ugly and awkward.

Her father was her primary source of affection and comfort, but he was unreliable and had his own problems. He broke many of his promises to her, he threatened suicide three times, and he finally had to be hospitalized for his alcohol problem.

When she was eight, her mother died of diphtheria, and she and her two younger brothers were sent to live with their stern and proper grandmother who was a strict disciplinarian and demanded perfection from her. Her grandmother taught her to hide her feelings and cry only in private.

Her father's visits became less and less frequent until he, too, died when she was almost ten. Losing both her parents left her with a sense of being abandoned and unloved that haunted her for many years.

Since there was very little love in her grandmother's home and because she always felt like an outsider there, she created a dream world to compensate for her loneliness and unhappiness.

Her feelings of loneliness and insecurity persisted until she was fifteen when she was sent to a boarding school in England.

There her life changed dramatically. She still found grammar and arithmetic difficult, but her confidence in herself began to soar.

She later said that it seemed she was always afraid of something: of the dark, of displeasing people, of authority, of failure. But there at her boarding school, all her fears left her for the first time in her life. It was there that she was taught to think for herself and to look at the world around her in a different way. Social graces and physical beauty were unimportant and, instead, a critical mind and a willingness to help others were emphasized.

But she again became her shy, insecure self when she returned to her grandmother's home. Intelligence and friendliness—the qualities that had distinguished her at school—were not those valued at home. And she once more became awkward and inhibited.

Just before her debutante party at age eighteen, one of her aunts told her that she was the "ugly duckling" of the family and would probably never have any boyfriends. This only confirmed the feelings of shame and inadequacy she had always felt.

After her positive experiences at her boarding school, she very much wanted to continue her education and go to college, but her grandmother said no. She was expected to fulfill her "social obligations and responsibilities" instead.

Since she felt out of place at society functions, she began to search instead for friendships based on her interest in social concerns.

As a woman:

She decided to compensate for her homely looks and her feelings of inferiority by becoming useful to people, so she began to emphasize intellectual achievement and social responsibility in her life.

She also learned that she had to conquer her own fears before she could reach out to help other people, so she began her own personal campaign to overcome her fears and feelings of inadequacy.

She later said, "You gain strength, courage, and confidence by every experience in which you really stop to look fear in the face. You must do the thing you cannot do."

She married a distant cousin and became an invaluable social adviser to him all his political life. When he was paralyzed by polio in 1921, she dedicated her life to his purposes and became eyes and ears for him, as well as a tireless reporter.

When he was elected president of the United States, she worked with him to obtain much-needed educational and social reform during the difficult years of the 1930s. She also revolutionized the role of the first lady and elevated the American woman to a new level of public consciousness.

She defied the segregation laws in 1939 when she sat between whites and blacks at the Southern Conference for Human Welfare in Birmingham, Alabama. And in July 1940 she made an impromptu speech at the Democratic National Convention, which helped her husband win an unprecedented third term as president.

After her husband's death in 1945, President Harry Truman named her a US delegate to the United Nations General Assembly. She served as chairperson of the UN's Human Rights Commission from 1947 to 1952, and the Universal Declaration of Human Rights adopted in 1948 was largely her work.

In 1951 a national poll named her "the greatest living American woman." Not only did she write many books, but she also became a popular public speaker and wrote a syndicated newspaper column called "My Day" for many years.

In 1961 President John F. Kennedy reappointed her to the United Nations and appointed her as the first chairperson of the President's Commission on the Status of Women. And she also served as an adviser to his newly founded Peace Corps.

She was the niece of one president and the wife of another, but she is remembered in her own right as a world leader in the fight for human rights and social reform. A famous public figure once honored her by stating: "No woman has ever so comforted the distressed or so distressed the comfortable."

When she died of tuberculosis at age seventy-eight in 1962, Adlai Stevenson said at her memorial service: "She would rather light candles than curse the darkness and her glow warmed the world."

"One's philosophy is best expressed not in words but in the choices one makes in daily living."

—Eleanor Roosevelt (1884–1962)

Georgia **O'Keeffe**

She was almost suspended from school.

As a girl:

She was born on a Wisconsin farm in 1887, the second of seven children. Right from the very beginning, she was keenly aware of colors and patterns that others around her didn't even notice.

She wanted to touch and feel everything, and when she was very young, she put dirt in her mouth to see what it tasted like.

She was also a very independent child with a mind of her own. If her sisters wore ribbons, she didn't. And if they wore their hair up, she wanted to wear hers down.

Even though she had brothers and sisters to play with, she often preferred to play alone with her dolls. She enjoyed making doll clothes for them and devised a collapsible doll-house that she could carry around on the farm.

She preferred her father's love of the land to her mother's love of books and spent a great deal of time outdoors, where she grew up independent and free spirited. Nature became an important part of her life and later her work.

When she was eleven, she and her sisters took private art lessons, but she grew tired of the lessons because her teacher insisted that her students copy pictures from a stack of prints she kept in a cupboard.

At home, she painted the imaginary scenes she really wanted to paint. She liked experimenting with shading and light and mixing colors to get just the right effect.

By the time she was thirteen, she knew she wanted to be an artist and took art lessons all through high school. She resented it when her teachers touched up her paintings because she wanted other people to see things just as she saw them.

When her family moved to Virginia her last two years of high school, she was enrolled at a boarding school for girls.

In Virginia she was quite different from the more traditionally feminine southern girls who wore frilly dresses with ruffles and bows and spent much of their time thinking and talking about boys. Georgia preferred to dress plainly and gave boys very little thought. While the other girls were encouraged to be passive and submissive, Georgia continued to be the same independent, self-assertive person she had always been.

It didn't take long for the other girls to be drawn to her strong personality and her mischievous nature. She sketched caricatures of the teachers, taught the other girls how to play poker, stayed up past her curfew, and went for long unchaperoned walks in the country, which weren't allowed at the time.

She had never been willing to live her life according to rules that made no sense to her, and she was not about to begin now. At one point, she would have been expelled if she had earned just one more demerit.

The other girls chose Georgia to be the art editor of the school's first yearbook, and her watercolor painting of red and yellow corn won the school's art prize.

As a woman:

During her college years, she went first to the Art Institute of Chicago and then later to an art school in New York City, but she always felt something was missing.

She did well in New York and won a scholarship for a prize still life, but she felt her work was not really her own. She longed to paint what was important to *her* and in her own way.

When she later took a painting class at the University of Virginia, she met a teacher named Alon Bement who spoke about art in a way Georgia had never heard before.

He told his students that it was most important to fill a space in a beautiful way. He gave his students exercises to do with different shapes and encouraged them to create their own designs. She began to experiment with the notion of abstract art and practiced filling the empty space with harmony and beauty.

Bement spoke about shades of color and flowing lines as a way to express feelings, and he even played music in his classes for his students to express visually on their canvases.

In the fall of 1915, Georgia took a position teaching art at a women's college in South Carolina to support herself and also to give her time to do her own work and discover her own style.

She stopped drawing the shapes and forms she had been taught and began to draw the shapes that she saw in her mind. She knew it was time for her to paint what she really wanted to paint.

Her pictures were no longer recognizable subjects like trees or flowers but were abstractions—lines and shapes created with different shades of black and white—all expressing her emotions.

Now that she had her own style, she was ready to put color back in her work. Always inspired by nature, flowers were one of her favorite subjects, and she painted them *large*, so that even busy New Yorkers would stop and appreciate their beauty.

She often found beauty in things that most people ignored or never even noticed, and she especially loved Texas, where the vast plains seemed to go on and on like the ocean.

She also loved the New Mexico desert, where she spent much of her time painting the stones and feathers found there as well as the bones left by decaying animals.

Although she knew many famous artists, she never copied their styles or joined their groups. Her paintings were like her children, and she expressed on canvas what she saw in her mind and felt in her heart.

She is not only one of the twentieth century's greatest painters, but she became an artist at a time when few women were encouraged to pursue their artistic talents.

Both her life and her work reflect her own personal integrity and courage to always be her own person.

Although she rarely signed her artwork, she left her mark on twentieth-century art in America and throughout the world.

"I found I could say things with color and shapes that I couldn't say in any other way—things I had no words for."
—Georgia O'Keeffe (1887–1986)

Jim **Thorpe**

His teacher called him "incorrigible."

As a boy:

Jim was born in 1887 in a log cabin in Oklahoma, and following the tradition of many Native Americans, his mother gave him and his twin brother both Indian as well as Christian names.

She named him Wa-tho-huck, meaning "Bright Path," not knowing just how prophetic a name that would be as he later became a world-famous athlete and probably the most renowned Native American of the twentieth century.

He inherited his love of athletics from his father and often said he had never seen another man who could match his father's strength and endurance.

At age six, he and his brother were sent to the reservation boarding school twenty-five miles away because their parents believed in a good education for their children.

But many of the white teachers at the reservation school were not properly trained nor were they very patient with the Indian children. One of his teachers even called him "incorrigible" because of his strong will and restless nature.

Having his twin brother there at school with him helped make life bearable in spite of his homesickness. Unfortunately, at age nine, his brother died from pneumonia and smallpox and Jim was grief stricken.

Without his brother at school, he was more miserable than ever and asked to drop out of school and work full time on the family farm, but his father insisted that he remain at school.

After breakfast one morning, Jim left school and walked the twenty-five miles home, only to have his father immediately return him to school in their horse-drawn wagon.

As soon as his father left, however, he defiantly struck out for home again, this time taking an alternative route that cut several miles off the trip. In an amazing display of endurance, he ran almost the whole way and actually beat his father home.

His father decided the only alternative was to send him to a school farther away. So at age eleven, Jim was sent to the Haskell Institute, an American Indian school in Lawrence, Kansas, hundreds of miles from his home.

While at Haskell, he developed his natural athletic skills, and his strong will seemed to have no limits. He was willing to try anything and do whatever was necessary to succeed.

When he was thirteen, he learned that his father had been injured in a hunting accident, so he hopped a freight train he thought was headed for Oklahoma but was actually headed in the opposite direction. When he realized his mistake, he jumped off the train and ended up walking 270 miles to get home.

His mother died in 1901 and, except for a brief time in Texas where he found work mending fences and taming wild horses, he spent the next four years at home, helping out on the farm and going to a one-room public school just three miles from home.

When he was almost seventeen, his athletic ability helped him gain admission to the Carlisle Indian School in Pennsylvania.

As a man:

Much of Jim's excellent physical conditioning as an adult came from the lessons he learned as a child from his father and the other Indian men who stressed the importance of strong bodies and good sportsmanship.

At Carlisle, Coach Glenn "Pop" Warner immediately recognized Jim's talents, and by the time Jim left Carlisle, he had earned varsity letters in eleven sports: boxing, wrestling, lacrosse, gymnastics, swimming, hockey, handball, basketball, football, track, and baseball. He also developed a thoroughly professional attitude toward athletics that he retained his entire life.

During his years at Carlisle, the school became a powerhouse in college football, even defeating football greats such as Harvard, the defending national champion at the time.

Jim was a superb field goal kicker, and as a runner, he had a unique combination of speed and strength that enabled him to run through tacklers as well as away from them.

A powerful runner, an accurate kicker, and a terror on defense, he was named an All-American in football in 1911 and again in 1912. In 1912 he scored twenty-five touchdowns.

The year 1912 also witnessed his greatest feat: winning two gold medals in the 1912 Olympic Games in Stockholm, Sweden.

He became the only man ever to win both the decathlon and the pentathlon, and he set a new world record by earning 8,412 points, almost 700 points more than the second-place finisher.

He returned to Carlisle a hero and was hailed by our entire country as "The World's Greatest Athlete."

After he left Carlisle, he signed with the New York Giants baseball club. Then in 1915 he also began his professional football career, playing football during the fall months and returning to baseball in the spring.

He was not only one of the greatest stars of professional football in its early years but also one of the most popular. In 1920 he became the first president of the American Professional Football Association (later to become the NFL).

In 1950 the Associated Press named him the "Greatest Football Player" as well as the "Greatest Male Athlete" of half a century.

In 1925 he announced his retirement from sports and was offered a job as a lecturer on a nationwide tour of schools. This gave him the opportunity to talk to students about the value of sports and also about Native American culture—both matters very dear to his heart. During his lecture tours, he stressed the importance of physical fitness for both boys and girls, believing it was an important factor in preventing juvenile delinquency.

His athletic greatness has stood the test of time, and he will be remembered as a legendary athlete for all centuries. The legend of Wa-tho-huck does indeed live forever!

"Athletics give you a fighting spirit to battle your problems of life, and they build sportsmanship."

—Jim Thorpe (1887–1953)

Norman Vincent **Peale**

AP Photo

As a boy:

He was born in a rural Ohio town in 1898, the son of a Methodist pastor who was also a physician.

Norman was painfully shy as a young boy and would run and hide in the attic whenever he saw visitors coming to the house so that he wouldn't have to recite poetry for them.

He was also thin for his age and lacked his younger brother's more rugged and athletic build, which made Norman somewhat self-conscious about his physical appearance.

He admired his father a great deal, but being the son of a pastor was not always easy. Sometimes the other kids teased him because he was a "p.k." (preacher's kid), and because he was a "p.k.," his teachers always expected exemplary behavior from him.

It was during his adolescence that he really began to develop a terrible inferiority complex, and he began telling himself that he would never amount to anything.

When he realized that everybody was beginning to agree with his negative self-appraisal, he began to feel even worse. He was tired of being so shy, so filled with self-doubt, and living like a scared rabbit, but he didn't know what to do about the inferiority complex that was making his life so miserable.

During high school he tried to earn some extra money by selling pots and pans and drove to another part of town where nobody knew him. But he became so flustered during his first attempt to sell something that he got right back into his car and drove back home.

Both his parents were strong, extroverted people who had made so many of his decisions for him that he had difficulty making even small decisions for himself.

His first semester of college he didn't earn a single A or B, and his second semester he did miserably in Greek, got an F in gym, and his only bright spot was an A in oratory.

He left college during his freshman year and returned home to enlist in the army, but his parents refused to let him enlist and sent him right back to college.

At the end of his freshman year, his mother also told him that he would have to improve his grades if he ever wanted to amount to anything.

He still continued to be plagued by agonizing self-consciousness when called upon to recite in class and often became confused, tongue-tied, and red-faced from embarrassment.

He described himself as "having the biggest inferiority complex in the state of Ohio." Then one day an event occurred that changed his life.

After class, his economics professor had a no-nonsense talk with him. He told Norman that his self-consciousness was really mostly self-centeredness and that it was time for him to get over his shyness and inferiority complex and become a man.

He also told him that, being a minister's son, he should know where to go for help.

As a man:

Norman decided to take his professor's advice and had a long talk with God about his problem. He asked God to help him work it out and, although his shyness never went away completely, it improved a great deal.

He wasn't sure he wanted to be a minister like his father, so following his graduation from college, he decided to try working for a newspaper.

After working for the newspaper for a year, he returned to school. In spite of his intention not to become a minister, he found he liked theology, and in 1924 he graduated from the School of Theology at Boston University.

He was beginning to gain a reputation not only as an excellent orator but also as a minister who could simplify the Word of God so that everyone could understand it.

He decided to try his hand at writing a book but became so discouraged that he threw his manuscript into the wastebasket. His wife, however, rescued the manuscript from the wastebasket and sent it to a publisher. The book was later called *A Guide to Confident Living* and made the best-seller list. Over the next four years it went through twenty-five printings.

By this time he was becoming much in demand as a public speaker and had received numerous honorary degrees from various colleges and universities.

In 1952 his book *The Power of Positive Thinking* was published, and it was unequaled in sales by any book except the Bible. It remained on the best-seller list for many years and was translated into twenty-three languages.

In the 1960s a motion picture was released, called *One Man's Way*, based on his biography, and it has been shown in many television reruns across the nation.

He was the minister of the Marble Collegiate Church in New York City where he spoke to three thousand people every Sunday. And he was also the coeditor with his wife of the inspirational monthly magazine *Guideposts*, which is read by millions of people.

He was the president and cofounder of the American Foundation of Religion and Psychiatry, which combined both religion and psychiatry in the treatment of people's problems, and he established a School of Practical Christianity for pastors to give them the opportunity to be enriched and refreshed spiritually.

On March 26, 1984, he was awarded the Presidential Medal of Freedom at the White House and told that "few Americans have contributed so much to the personal happiness of their fellow citizens."

By the time he retired from the ministry in 1984, he had come a long way: from a young man with a terrible inferiority complex to being one of America's most influential, most popular, and most loved preachers.

"Trust God and live one day at a time."
—Norman Vincent Peale (1898–1993)

Chien-Shiung **Wu**

She wanted an education.

As a girl:

Chien-Shiung was born in China in 1912 in a small town where there was no school for girls, so her father started one. He believed in equal rights for women and wanted her to have the very best education possible.

Their home was always filled with newspapers, magazines, and books, and in the evenings, the family read together. Her father encouraged her and her two brothers to ask questions and to solve problems, and her mother urged other parents to give their daughters an education and to stop binding their feet.

Her father's school was the only girls' school in the region, and at that time, it had classes only for girls up to age nine.

Most of her classmates did not go on to high school, but she wanted a full education, and since her parents believed that girls should be as well educated as boys, they enrolled her in a boarding school in Soochow some distance away.

Two types of education were offered at this school: teacher training and academic studies. She enrolled in the teachers course because it was free and its graduates were assured jobs.

But as she began to realize that her friends taking the academic course were learning far more about science and foreign languages, she persuaded them to lend her their books each night after they finished their homework. Studying far into the night, she taught herself physics, chemistry, and mathematics.

While she was in high school at Soochow, she became the leader of the underground student movement there, which urged the Chinese political leaders to stand firm against the Japanese.

She graduated from Soochow in 1930 with the highest grades in her class and was offered a place at China's elite National Central University at Nanjing.

There, too, she worked so hard that she became the university's top student. Once when a group of professors met together, they bragged to each other about their best student. Later, they learned that each professor had been bragging about the same student—Chien-Shiung.

She believed in hard work and once said, "You must work very hard at the beginning. It is hard to push the door open and get inside a subject. But once you understand it, it is very interesting."

After graduating with her bachelor's degree in 1934, she taught for a year. Then she took a research job at the National Academy of Sciences in Shanghai where she was encouraged by her instructor to earn her PhD in the United States.

In 1936 she sailed for the United States, planning to work for her PhD in physics and then return home, but she never saw her family again.

Japan invaded China the following year, and her family told her to stay in America until it was safe to come home. By the time she returned to China in 1973 for a visit, her parents and brothers were all dead.

As a woman:

She became well known as a physicist in the United States and was an expert on fission (the splitting of the nucleus of an atom into two parts). The first atomic bomb had not yet been created, but scientists had done much of the groundwork, including research on fission.

She was not asked to join the team of scientists that was designing the atomic bomb because, at that time, physics was still thought of as a man's subject. At some universities, women were not even allowed to study physics.

During World War II these attitudes changed because there was a shortage of physicists, so women were hired. She was appointed to teach physics at Princeton University, the first woman to hold that position.

Finally in 1944, she was asked to join the team building the atomic bomb. Working at Columbia University in New York, she helped design the radiation detectors for the bomb.

After the war, she remained at Columbia where she was greatly respected for her high standards and hard work. Some of her students called her "The Dragon Lady" because she expected them to work as hard as she did.

In 1956 Dr. Tsung-Dao Lee and Dr. Chen Ning Yang asked her to help them discover why the tiny particles inside an atom might not always act according to the laws of nature.

She lined up a research team in Washington, DC, and six months later her team had found the answer. Dr. Lee and Dr. Yang were awarded a Nobel Prize in physics for this discovery, which disproved a long-standing law of physics, and she was very disappointed that she was not included in the prize.

But she followed the advice her father had given her as a young girl, "Ignore the obstacles. Just put your head down and keep walking forward," so soon she was "walking forward" with new research projects.

She truly loved her work, and she once said that "there is only one thing worse than coming home from the lab to a sink full of dirty dishes, and that is not going to the lab at all."

By the time she retired in 1981, she was known as one of the world's leading physicists, and her careful experiments and dedicated work had brought her many awards and honors, including the Wolf Prize in Physics and the National Medal of Science. She was also the first living scientist to have an asteroid named after her.

After her retirement, she traveled extensively, giving lectures and encouraging more women to become scientists. She was the world's most distinguished woman physicist of her time and was named "The Queen of Physics" by *Newsweek* magazine (1963).

Even after her death in 1997, she still remains a legend among physicists and an inspiration to all who aspire to invent, to experiment, and to challenge the scientific status quo.

"Just put your head down and keep walking forward."
—Chien-Shiung Wu (1912–1997)

Jackie **Robinson**

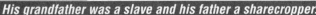

His grandfather was a slave and his father a sharecropper.

AP Photo

As a boy:

He was born in a small farm-house near Cairo, Georgia, in 1919, the youngest of five children. His grandfather had been a slave and his father was a share-cropper (sharecroppers had to give half of the crops they grew as rent to the owner of the farm).

When Jackie was only six months old, his father deserted the family and moved to another state. Without his father to work the farm, Jackie and his family had to leave the farm.

In 1920 Jackie and his family moved to Pasadena, California, where they shared a small apartment with his uncle. His mother took in washing to pay her way, and Jackie often ate day-old bread dipped in milk and sugar for supper.

Somehow his mother was able to save a little money, and a welfare agency helped her buy a small house. Some of their white neighbors called the children ugly names and even threw rocks at them. But even though they tried to make the family move, Jackie's mother refused to let their racial taunts drive her away.

His mother expected her children to do well in school, and although Jackie was a good student, his heart was always more into sports and games than in his schoolwork.

After school he hauled junk, shined shoes, and sold newspapers to make money. He also hung out with a local gang and was headed for trouble until two men changed his life.

The first was a local mechanic who took an interest in him and convinced him that if he continued with the gang, he would end up hurting his mother as well as himself. The other man was the pastor of his church who became his friend and counselor and helped channel his energy into sports.

Jackie played all sports, and he played them well. He won the city championship the first time he took up Ping-Pong, and he became a four-sport star at his high school—earning letters in football, track, baseball, and basketball.

At Pasadena Junior College in 1938 he set a new broad jump record of twenty-five feet, six and one-half inches in the morning, and then in the afternoon he changed into his baseball uniform. Playing shortstop, he helped his team win the league championship. His football and basketball teams also won league titles, and college coaches rushed to offer him athletic scholarships.

Jackie chose the University of California at Los Angeles (UCLA), which was close to his home. Football was his first love in those days, and he played halfback and safety on UCLA's unbeaten 1939 team.

After the season ended, he moved on to basketball, track, and baseball. He played well enough to become UCLA's first four-letter man.

In the spring of 1941 he quit school because he wanted to begin earning money to help his mother, and he wasn't sure a college degree would really help a black man get a good job.

On December 7, 1941, the Japanese bombed Pearl Harbor and six months later he received his draft notice to serve his country.

As a man:

The army sent him to Fort Riley, Kansas, where he completed his basic training and applied for Officers' Candidate School (OCS). But the army was not accepting black officer candidates.

Jackie complained to Joe Louis, the world heavyweight boxing champion, who also happened to be at Fort Riley at the time. Soon after that, Jackie's orders for OCS came through, and he graduated in 1943 as a second lieutenant.

After his discharge from the army in 1944, he wanted to play baseball, but at that time, there were no African Americans playing on any of the major league teams.

He joined the Kansas City Monarchs, a Negro League team, where he continued to encounter as much racial discrimination as in the army. Many hotels and restaurants refused to serve black people, so he and his teammates often slept and ate on the bus.

But in New York, one man was planning to break baseball's color barrier. Branch Rickey, owner of the Brooklyn Dodgers, had decided it was time to end segregation in baseball.

Rickey knew that the first black Dodger would be abused by fans and players alike, so the man would have to be more than just a great baseball player. He would have to be a great human being.

In 1945 Rickey decided that Jackie was that man! Jackie knew it would be hard, but he accepted the challenge because he hoped he could help open doors for all black men everywhere.

Jackie joined the Montreal Royals, the Dodgers' top minor league team, and though taunted by fans, he never lost his cool.

Rickey decided it was time to move Jackie up to the major leagues. April 15, 1947, was a historic day for major league baseball and for the entire nation. When the major league season opened that day, Jackie was there in the Dodger lineup, the first African American to play baseball for a major league team.

In the beginning, his white teammates were cool toward him, but as the fans and opposing players abused Jackie with catcalls and racial taunts, his teammates united behind him.

Jackie answered the abuse with his bat and his feet. His .297 batting average helped the Dodgers win the pennant, and he led the league in stolen bases. He was also named National League Rookie of the Year. Then in 1949 he was named the league's Most Valuable Player (MVP) and also starred in a movie about his life.

In 1957 he retired from baseball with a lifetime batting average of .311, and in 1962 he was voted into the National Baseball Hall of Fame, the first black man to receive baseball's highest honor.

After his retirement, he continued to speak out whenever he saw injustice and worked hard for equal rights for all Americans. His courageous example paved the way for the full integration of major league baseball in the years that followed.

Rickey had chosen well. Jackie was not only a great ballplayer, he was also a great human being!

"The first freedom for all people is freedom of choice."
—Jackie Robinson (1919–1972)

Maya **Angelou**

AP Photo

As a girl:

She was born Marguerite Johnson in St. Louis, Missouri, in 1928. When she was about three years old, her parents divorced, and she and her four-year-old brother Bailey were sent to live with their grandmother in Stamps, Arkansas.

Growing up in Stamps, Marguerite learned what it was like to be a black girl in a world whose boundaries were set by whites. It meant having to wear old hand-me-down clothes from white women and not being permitted to be treated by a white doctor.

As a child, she saw herself as a "too-big Negro girl with nappy black hair, broad feet, and a space between her teeth that would hold a number-two pencil." She dreamed of waking to find her "nappy black hair" metamorphosed to a long blond bob because she felt life was better for a white girl than for a black girl.

After living with their grandmother for several years, she and her brother returned to St. Louis to live with their mother, who was working part time as a card dealer in a gambling parlor.

At age eight, Marguerite was raped by her mother's boyfriend, and after she testified at his trial, he was found murdered. She felt responsible for his death because of her testimony at his trial and vowed never to speak in public again.

She felt so bad that she did indeed become mute and spoke to no one but Bailey. Finally, she was sent back to Stamps because no one knew what to do to help her.

Even though she did not speak in public for years, she listened intently to everything that went on around her. Many people thought she was retarded and openly talked about her as if she didn't understand what they were saying. But her grandmother never became discouraged or gave up on her.

When she was ten years old, she met Bertha Flowers, the most educated black woman in Stamps. Bertha Flowers not only read books with her, but she also gave her a poetry book and told her that "a person who truly loves poetry reads it aloud." For the first time in years, Marguerite began to believe in herself again and began to speak.

By the time she graduated from the eighth grade with honors in 1940, she was talking as if she had never stopped, and people now began to see her as precocious and eloquent.

But she still had to deal with the racism that surrounded her. When she developed a painful tooth problem, she and her grandmother had to travel twenty-five miles by Greyhound bus because there were no black dentists in

Stamps, and the white dentist refused to treat any black people—not even a black child in pain.

Later in 1940 she and her brother were sent to San Francisco to live with their mother again, and Marguerite became pregnant. At the age of sixteen she delivered her son Clyde, three weeks after graduating from high school.

She eventually returned to Stamps with her son but could not readjust to the racial bias in the South. She left again after being warned that the Ku Klux Klan might come calling.

As a woman:

After leaving Stamps, she returned to San Francisco and moved into her mother's fourteen-room house where her brother Bailey was also living.

There followed many years of struggle and heartache as she struggled to support herself and her child. She worked hard to build a career as a dancer, singer, actress, and finally a writer.

In the beginning, she tried many jobs, but none of them lasted long. While working in a restaurant, one of her jobs was to drive the owner's prize fighters to their fights. But she was quickly fired when she tried to stop one of the fights because she didn't want to see her friend get hurt.

By the time she was twenty-two, she had decided she wanted to use her creative talents to make a living. After working as a dancer for a short time, she auditioned as a singer at the Purple Onion, a famous San Francisco nightclub. She was hired and, at the age of twenty-six, her last name was changed to Angelou.

She later joined the chorus of the popular black folk opera *Porgy and Bess* and traveled to twenty-two countries. But when Clyde got sick, she left the cast and returned to her mother's home to take care of him.

Now she was out of a job again, her brother was in prison for selling stolen goods, and she became seriously depressed. A musician friend persuaded her to be grateful for all the good things in her life, rather than sad about the bad things, and she slowly came out of her depression and began to write.

At age forty-two, her humorous autobiographical account about growing up in segregated Arkansas, *I Know Why the Caged Bird Sings*, was nominated for a National Book Award, and she became the first African American woman to make the nonfiction best-seller lists.

She has been able to use both her positive and her negative experiences in her poetry, and at age forty-three, her first volume of poetry, *Just Give Me a Cool Drink of Water 'fore I Diiie*, was published and nominated for a Pulitzer Prize.

She wrote and delivered a poem, "On the Pulse of the Morning," at President Bill Clinton's inauguration on January 20, 1993. He believed that her life and work embodied his brightest hopes for his administration: "An America in which individual potential triumphs over poverty, neglect, and racism."

As the first black woman director in Hollywood, she has written, produced, directed, and starred in productions for stage, film, and television. And as autobiographer and poet, she has transformed the raw material of often-painful experience into some of the most moving works in American literature.

She is an author, poet, historian, songwriter, playwright, dancer, stage and screen producer, director, performer, singer, and civil rights activist.

"You might encounter many defeats but you must never be defeated, ever."

—Maya Angelou (1928–   )

Martin Luther **King Jr.**

His friends weren't allowed to play with him.

As a boy:

Martin was born on January 15, 1929, in Atlanta, Georgia, and grew up in a house close to the Ebenezer Baptist Church where his father was the minister and his mother the organist and music director.

When he was six and started school, his two best friends, the sons of the neighborhood grocer, were no longer allowed to play with him because they were white and he was black. This left a lasting impression on him that he remembered all his life.

While he was growing up, he experienced racial discrimination all around him. Black people could live only in black neighborhoods, and black children could only attend black schools. Black people could not use "white" restrooms or "white" drinking fountains, and black people were expected to sit in the back of the buses and give their seats to white people when there were no empty seats. And most black men were expected to take menial jobs such as janitor or garbage collector.

Once when Martin and his father were ordered to the back section of a shoe store reserved for black people, they refused to move to the back and left the store without buying any shoes.

While he was growing up, his parents had firm rules for their family: Martin and his brother and sister always had to be home for dinner to share in the family discussions, and they always had to treat other people with respect.

He was a sensitive boy who hated violence in any form and preferred to avoid unpleasant situations whenever possible. Once when a white woman in a store accused him of stepping on her foot and slapped him, he said nothing and just left the store.

He had his share of fights as a young boy, but he never used his fists. He did not like to fight at all, and if he could not talk his opponent out of fighting and it came down to physical combat, he would say, "Let's go to the grass" because he was an excellent wrestler.

He also had occasional skirmishes with his brother, whom he once knocked out when he hit him on the head with a telephone.

He was particularly close to his grandmother, and when his brother accidentally knocked her unconscious while sliding down a banister and they thought she was dead, Martin felt so bad that he jumped out a second-story window in his home. Fortunately, neither his grandmother nor he was seriously hurt.

He had always loved "big words," and he had a remarkable speaking vocabulary. As an eleventh grader, he entered an oratorical contest in Valdosta, Georgia, where his speech won a prize. But after the contest, his teacher and he had to stand up on the bus all the way back home to Atlanta because there were no seats in the back of the bus, and they were not allowed to sit in the empty seats up front in the "white" section.

When he was fifteen, he passed the admission exam and enrolled at Morehouse College in Atlanta, an all-male, all-black college and the alma mater of both his father and his grandfather.

As a man:

While at Morehouse, he was deeply influenced by Benjamin Mays, the president, whose quiet dignified preaching style was quite unlike the highly emotional style of Martin's father.

After graduating from Morehouse, he attended Pennsylvania's Crozer Theological Seminary, where he graduated at the top of his class with a bachelor's degree in divinity and a scholarship to the graduate school of his choice.

After earning his doctorate at Boston University, he returned to the South to begin his ministry in Montgomery, Alabama.

All his life he had been inspired by such black people as Harriet Tubman, Nat Turner, and Frederick Douglass and dreamed about also helping his people the way they had.

He combined the teachings of Jesus (who advocated loving your enemy), the teachings of Mahatma Gandhi (who advocated nonviolent rebellion against unjust causes), and the teachings of Henry David Thoreau (who advocated civil disobedience when justified by the situation), and he became the leader of a civil rights movement based on nonviolent resistance.

As he became increasingly more active in working for social reform, he led sit-ins, pray-ins, lobby-ins, boycotts, marches, and other nonviolent demonstrations for civil rights. He also organized voter registration drives and delivered inspiring speeches throughout the country.

"We Shall Overcome" was adopted as the Freedom Movement Song, and in 1963 he led the Civil Rights March on Washington with a quarter of a million people (more than half of them white). He called this march "the greatest demonstration for freedom in the history of the nation."

He delivered his famous "I have a dream" speech from the steps of the Lincoln Memorial, and despite threats to his life, he continued to work for his dream of equality and justice.

Time magazine named him "Man of the Year," and his picture was on the cover of its January 3, 1964, issue (the second black man to be so honored).

On July 2, 1964, the Civil Rights Bill, which he and other black leaders had helped draft, was passed and became law.

That same year he was also awarded the Nobel Peace Prize for his work in race relations—the youngest person, the third black person, and the twelfth American to be so honored.

After his assassination on April 4, 1968, in Memphis, Tennessee, people came from all over the world to attend his funeral. Both our country and the world honored this young black minister as no private citizen had ever been honored. American flags and flags of the United Nations flew at half mast in tribute to a man who had dedicated his life to trying to help his people.

Even after his death, his words and his example continue to inspire people, and we now celebrate a national holiday in his honor: Martin Luther King Day!

"I have a dream."

—Martin Luther King Jr. (1929–1968)

Sandra Day O'Connor

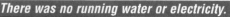
There was no running water or electricity.

AP Photo

As a girl:

Sandra was born in El Paso, Texas, in 1930, but moved shortly after her birth to the four-room family ranch house on the Arizona–New Mexico border. The family ranch at that time had no bathroom, no running water, no electricity, and no gas.

Her father was determined that his daughter would learn to ride and rope and shoot as well as any man, so he taught her how to ride a horse, drive a pickup truck, shoot jackrabbits, mend fences, and care for sick livestock.

Her mother, on the other hand, stressed the importance of educating her mind. From early childhood, her mother read to her, and from her mother Sandra learned to love books.

Because the ranch was so remote, she had no playmates during her early childhood, and so she spent much of her time with the ranch hands and the animals on the ranch. She always had a soft spot for stray kittens, crippled birds, and even baby mice.

By 1937 her family was doing well enough to build a separate bunkhouse for their herdsmen (who had been sleeping on the front porch) and install indoor plumbing in the main house.

Still, times were very hard because of the high temperatures and severe drought throughout the southern, central, and western states. Millions of acres of once-fertile land became dry and parched. It was the worst drought in American history.

The central United States soon came to be known as the Dust Bowl and left farmers and ranchers without a means of supporting their families because they could not grow crops.

No longer able to make a living from the land, many people moved farther west or north to seek a better life, and thousands of people lost their farms and land in bank foreclosures.

Those times were hard for everyone, and Sandra's father kept five hundred dollars in a safe-deposit box as an emergency fund in case he and his family had to leave their ranch.

Finally, the federal government established a program that paid ranchers twelve dollars apiece for dying cattle and twenty dollars a head for those worth shipping to market. This was less than they were paid before the drought, but it was enough to help them survive.

Since the local schools were not as good as the schools in El Paso, Sandra moved to El Paso to stay with her grandparents.

During her years at an all-girls' school, she received not only an excellent education but she also developed the public-speaking skills that helped her so much later in life. The friends she made there are still her friends to this day.

She learned a great deal from both her parents. From her mother, she learned to be gracious and dignified even under trying conditions. And from her father, she learned common sense, honesty, fair play, and self-sufficiency.

She was an excellent student who made top grades, and upon graduating from high school in 1946, she applied to only one college—Stanford University in California.

As a woman:

She graduated magna cum laude from Stanford in 1950 and third in her class from the Stanford Law School in 1952.

While at Stanford she studied long and hard and was named an editor of the *Stanford Law Review*. As an editor, she spent countless hours in the library editing manuscripts and checking articles for facts, which taught her the importance of meticulous preparation and thorough research.

After graduating from law school, finding a job was not easy because so many law firms were reluctant to hire women back then.

She finally found a position as a law clerk in the office of the San Mateo, California, county attorney. She soon found that public employment offered her a greater range of duties, more responsibility, and a broader knowledge of law than she could ever have gotten working for a private law firm.

Between 1960 and 1965 she stayed home to raise her family of three sons while still maintaining her contacts in the legal world through her volunteer work.

In 1965 she became an Arizona assistant attorney general, and in 1969 she was appointed to the Arizona state senate.

Despite her support for laws that gave women greater equality, she was also a strong advocate for the traditional values of motherhood and family.

In 1970 she was elected to the Arizona state senate, where she served two terms, but in 1974 she announced that she would not seek a third term as a state senator. She had decided it was time to leave politics and return to what she loved most—the law.

She was easily elected judge of the Arizona Superior Court in 1974 where she gained a reputation as a formidable judge who expected the attorneys who appeared in her courtroom to be as well prepared and hardworking as she was.

She also gained a reputation for her competence and fairness on the bench, and in 1978 US Senator Barry Goldwater and the Arizona Republican Party invited her to run for governor. She reluctantly refused, feeling that she should stay on the superior court bench where she felt she could do the most good.

In 1979 she was appointed to the Arizona Court of Appeals where she no longer worked alone as she had as a trial judge. Now she was one of three judges working together toward each decision.

Then in 1981 she made history by becoming the first woman appointed to the US Supreme Court. After being nominated by President Ronald Reagan, her nomination was unanimously confirmed by the US Senate.

In 1988 she was treated for breast cancer, and some thought she might retire from the bench. But she saw the cancer not as an obstacle but as just another "stepping-stone" in her life.

She continued to carry a full workload and has become a model of personal integrity for all of us—always voting her conscience, even when sometimes it was not the popular way to go.

"One small voice can make a difference."
—Sandra Day O'Connor (1930–   )

Toni **Morrison**

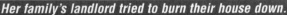

Her family's landlord tried to burn their house down.

AP Photo/Hyperion Books for Children, Dwight Carter

As a girl:

Chloe Anthony Wofford was born in 1931 in Lorain, Ohio, part of a large black community near the Underground Railroad (a network of people who had helped thousands of slaves escape to freedom in the North and Canada).

Her maternal grandparents had been sharecroppers in Alabama, but Chloe's parents moved north to Lorain, Ohio, to escape the racism of the South.

Her mother grew up to be a patient but determined woman. When an eviction notice was put on their house, she tore it off. And when there were maggots in the flour, she wrote a letter to President Franklin Roosevelt.

Her father, a shipyard welder, was a hardworking man, but because he had had bad experiences with white people, he distrusted all white men and did his best to keep white people out of his life.

As Chloe grew older, she heard many family stories about discrimination and injustice, but there was one story in particular that left a lasting impression.

Her family told how when she was two years old, they were unable to pay the monthly rent of four dollars, and their angry landlord tried to burn down the house with the family still inside. That story about hatred was a story she would remember all her life and would later include in her writing.

Even though her family lived in an integrated neighborhood and she attended an integrated school, African Americans were still barred from some places in town such as the lake in the city park where only white children were allowed to swim.

Her family was proud of their heritage, and storytelling was the main form of entertainment for her family. It was there she heard the songs and tales of southern black folklore that she later used in her writings.

She loved to read, and the family often spent some of its hard-earned money on books. Her mother belonged to a book club, and she remembers how excited she was whenever a new book arrived.

At age thirteen, she got a job cleaning house for a white family after school to help with the family expenses. When she complained to her father that the work was hard and the woman was mean, he reminded her that she didn't live there. He told her that she should just go do her job, get her money, and come home. Dignity and diligence were important family values in her home.

Even though the family was poor, Chloe's parents made the children feel very important, and her father taught her to always have pride in her work.

He told her how whenever he welded a perfect seam, he signed his name to it even though no one else would ever see it. Chloe followed his example and always tried to do her very best.

She was an excellent student, and when she graduated with honors in 1949 from Lorain High School, she became the first woman in her family to go to college.

As a woman:

After enrolling at Howard University in Washington, DC, she shortened her middle name Anthony to Toni, and from then on, everyone called her Toni.

While traveling with the campus theater group through the South, she experienced firsthand the racial discrimination and injustices she had heard about before in her family's stories.

After receiving a bachelor's degree in English from Howard University in 1953 and a master's degree in English from Cornell University in 1955, she taught for several years.

She married in 1958, but it was not a happy marriage. She joined a writing group to ease her unhappiness, and for one of her assignments, she wrote a story about a little African American girl she remembered from her childhood who had wanted blue eyes. She wrote about the whole issue of physical beauty and the pain that comes from wanting to be someone else.

In 1965 she accepted an editorial job with the Random House publishing office in Syracuse, New York, and moved there with her two sons. While in Syracuse she continued to work on the story she had written earlier about the little black girl who wanted blue eyes. She wrote in her spare time and found great enjoyment from creating her own world through her writing.

Recognizing her talent as an editor, Random House transferred her to its New York City office in 1968 where she

71

became a senior editor—the only black woman to hold such a position at that time.

She became a well-respected editor and remained with Random House until 1983. When she realized there were very few books written about black women and girls, she decided to work seriously on the story she had begun years earlier and rewrite it as a novel. Her novel *The Bluest Eye* was published in 1970.

By this time she was gaining national recognition for her essays, articles, and book reviews in well-known newspapers and magazines. She published her second novel, *Sula*, in 1973, a novel that examines the importance of friendships between black women.

Her next book, *Song of Solomon*, was about a young black man discovering the richness of his ancestry and became a national best-seller when it was published in 1977.

Then came *Tar Baby* (1981), which appeared on the *New York Times* best-seller list less than a month after it was published and remained there for four months.

Her novel *Beloved* (1987) made a powerful statement about slavery and won the Pulitzer Prize for Fiction in 1988. Then in 1993 she received the Nobel Prize for Literature, the eighth woman and the first black woman to ever receive the prize.

She is one of literature's greatest women, but she has never forgotten her students. Even on the day she received the news about being awarded the Nobel Prize, she still returned to teach her classes at Princeton University.

"I take teaching as seriously as I do my writing."
—Toni Morrison (1931–   )

Bill **Cosby**

AP Photo

As a boy:

He was born in 1937 in Philadelphia, Pennsylvania, and times were hard. As a boy, Bill saw less and less of his father. Eventually his father disappeared altogether, leaving the family to fend for themselves.

His mother went to work as a maid, working twelve hours a day, while Bill pitched in after school, hitting the streets with the shoeshine kit he had made out of empty orange crates. He also took care of the rest of the family until his mother got home from work every evening.

From the age of nine, he always had a job of some kind. And when he was eleven, he spent the summer clerking at a grocery store twelve hours a day, six days a week for eight dollars a week.

His mother was the major influence in his life, and in spite of her long hours at work, she always found time to read to her children. And even when there was no money for toys or Christmas presents, his mother always gave them a lot of love.

The other major influence in his life was his paternal grandfather, who loved to tell stories and encouraged Bill to hone his own storytelling skills.

One Christmas Eve when there was no money for any presents or a Christmas tree, Bill improvised a Christmas tree of his own and entertained his family by telling stories.

Telling funny stories came naturally to him, and he became not only the family comedian but also the class comic. Telling funny stories became a way of making friends, and he used his wit to compensate for his being a poor student and not always listening to the teacher.

His cleverness even saved him from bodily harm more than a few times—like the time he told a gang of boys that the Salvation Army was giving out free ice cream just up the street, so the guys took off instead of beating up Bill and his friend.

Although he was very bright, he was an underachiever in school and dropped out of school in the tenth grade. He worked briefly as a shoe repairman's apprentice, but that job didn't last long when his employer failed to see any humor in the way he amused himself by nailing women's high heels onto men's shoes.

He shined shoes for a while and even tried going to night school, but he was still too restless to apply himself to his schoolwork. At nineteen, he followed in his father's footsteps and joined the navy.

In the navy he was trained to do physical therapy with disabled navy and marine veterans from the Korean War. This became a turning point in his life when he saw some of the veterans struggling so hard for an education that he had never taken seriously. He decided to enroll in a correspondence course to complete his high school education.

When he passed the high school equivalency exam at the end of the course, he finally earned the treasured diploma that had eluded him for so long.

As a man:

After his four-year enlistment ended, he was determined to further his education, but now almost twenty-three, he wasn't sure anyone would be willing to take a chance on him.

While in the navy, he had been a member of the US Navy track team. Impressed by both Bill's athletic skills and his maturity, Temple University in Philadelphia offered him a full-tuition athletic scholarship.

During his sophomore year at Temple, while working part time as a bartender, he found himself telling amusing stories to his patrons. It wasn't long before the management asked him to fill in for the club's comedian when he failed to show up for work.

Word of his talent spread north to New York, and he landed a gig at the Gaslight, a Greenwich Village coffeehouse. He managed to juggle both his school work and his job until the summer break.

During his junior year he had to make the hardest decision of his life. Offered a choice gig at Philadelphia's Town Hall, he had to choose between school and comedy.

He chose show business and developed his own style of comedy, abandoning racial humor in favor of comedy monologues which used everyday situations that people could relate to.

At the peak of the civil rights movement, he was unique among black comedians of the time because he didn't use race as a subject. He chose to talk about universal similarities between the races rather than focus on the differences.

In 1965 he made the transition from stand-up comedian to actor when he became the first African American to star in a television series, *I Spy* (1965–1968), thereby breaking the racial barrier in television.

It was a historic moment with a black man and a white man working together as equals. It created international interest in the show and in the young comedian who won three Emmy Awards and helped advance the status of African Americans on television.

Feature films soon followed, and then he returned to television to star in his own sitcoms and a mystery series.

With their gentle humor and upbeat message, his sitcoms reached across racial boundaries and were watched and loved by everyone.

His message was constant: "'Race' is one thing, but it isn't the only one and it isn't always the primary one."

He revolutionized American comedy, but he is much more than an entertainer. He used his comedic talents to educate a nation by proving that color barriers can be dissolved and by showing that a style of humor based on universal human experiences rather than on racial tensions or stereotypes does indeed have a worldwide audience.

He was inducted into the Television Hall of Fame in 1984, but he has never forgotten what it's like to be poor. He has given both his time and his money to many social causes and educational institutions.

"I don't know the key to success, but the key to failure is trying to please everybody."

—Bill Cosby (1937–   )

Marian Wright **Edelman**

She was aware of racism and hated it.

As a girl:

Marian was born in the small town of Bennettsville, South Carolina, the youngest of five children, in 1939. And like most southern towns back then, it was segregated.

That meant that the African Americans lived in the poorer neighborhoods and were not allowed to vote, use the public library, play on the public playgrounds, drink from the same water fountains as whites, or swim in the town pool.

Classrooms were unheated, textbooks were falling apart, and students often had to share books because there weren't enough for everyone.

Both her father, a Baptist minister, and her mother, the church organist and choir director, instilled a strong work ethic in all their children and kept them busy either working, reading, or studying.

Study and community work: those were the parental doctrines that set Marian's life on its path in her early years. She learned that service was not something you did in your spare time. "It was the very purpose of life."

Children were taught by parental example that daily service, hard work, perseverance, and a capacity to struggle in the face of adversity were expected and that "giving up" was never an option.

They were urged by their parents to do their best in whatever task they took on. Homework had to be done every night, and if no homework was assigned, they were told to assign themselves homework. It was read, read, read.

Although her childhood and family life were very happy, the ugliness of racial prejudice was never far away.

One of Marian's childhood friends died after stepping on a nail and becoming seriously ill from the infection because he was unable to get the proper medical attention he needed.

And another classmate broke his neck jumping into the town creek from the bridge because only white children were allowed to swim in the public swimming pool.

She later learned that the creek where black people were allowed to swim and fish was the hospital sewage outlet.

Her dad died of a heart attack when she was fourteen, and as she rode with him in the ambulance, she listened carefully to his final words. He told her that she could be anything she wanted to be, and he again emphasized the importance of education, self-discipline, character, service, and determination.

Her dad died before the ambulance got to the hospital, but after his death, the family carried on just as he would have wanted them to—studying hard, working hard, and helping others.

By her last year in high school, Marian was the only child still at home, and her mother, who was already the director of the old folks home across from their church, reached out again into the community to take in foster children.

She graduated as the valedictorian for her class, and her yearbook prophecy foresaw her as a physician.

As a woman:

As a student at Spelman College in Atlanta, Georgia, the message was clear and much the same as her parents' message: education is for improving the lives of others and for leaving your community and world a better place than you found it.

While at Spelman, she received fellowships to live and study abroad. Then, following her return to the United States, she joined in some of the civil rights demonstrations. When she realized how many people needed legal help but could not afford it, she decided to become a lawyer.

After graduating from Spelman, she received a fellowship to Yale Law School, but she found it difficult to sit in her Yale law classes while others were working for civil rights full time.

During spring break in her third year of law school, she went to Greenwood, Mississippi, to help educate black people about their civil rights. The police attacked her and her coworkers with police dogs, and that experience only strengthened her resolve to become a lawyer and fight such abuses of the law.

She returned to Yale and finished law school, then immediately signed on as one of the first interns in a program sponsored by the NAACP (National Association for the Advancement of Colored People) Legal Defense and Education Fund. She trained in New York City and then moved to Mississippi, where she felt she could do the most good.

After working as a legal counselor for a year, she took the bar exam to become a lawyer and became the first black woman lawyer in Mississippi.

In 1968 she moved to Washington, DC, so that she could continue her work for the poor where it would do the most good—the nation's capital.

With a grant from the Field Foundation, she founded the Washington Research Project to report on the country's poor and underprivileged. Her goal was to be a voice for America's poor and to see that laws to protect them were enforced.

In 1973 the Washington Research Project became the Children's Defense Fund (CDF). With the name change and the new emphasis on children, she began to devote her full energies to the cause of the nation's fifty million children.

Her dedication to protecting children has been the driving force in her life. She considers children to be "our most fragile and precious resource."

She was now beginning to receive national recognition for her efforts to help children, and in 1983 the *Ladies Home Journal* named her one of the one hundred most influential women in America.

Many believe she is the single most effective spokesperson for child care in America today. An activist, lawyer, lecturer, wife, mother, and best-selling author, she has dedicated her life to those who cannot always lift themselves up.

"The measure of our worth is inside our heads and hearts and not outside in our possessions or on our backs."
—Marian Wright Edelman (1939–   )

Wilma **Rudolph**

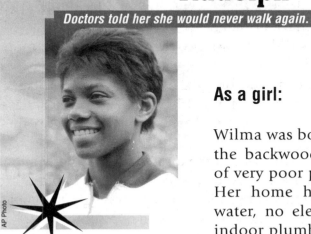

AP Photo

As a girl:

Wilma was born in a shack in the backwoods of Tennessee of very poor parents in 1940. Her home had no running water, no electricity, and no indoor plumbing.

She was born two months early and was a tiny, sickly baby, weighing only a little over four pounds. She was so frail that no one was even sure she would survive.

By age four she had been stricken with scarlet fever, chicken pox, measles, mumps, double pneumonia, and polio, which left one of her legs partially paralyzed. Doctors predicted she would never walk again.

Like other black families, her family had to deal with

prejudice. Black people could not sit with white people on buses, on trains, or in movie theaters. And black children and white children went to separate schools.

White doctors took care of white people, black doctors took care of black people, and there was only one black doctor for her town's entire black population.

The nearest hospital for black people was in Nashville, more than an hour's drive away, so twice each week Wilma and her mother traveled by bus to the hospital to get treatment for her leg.

Back home, her family helped her massage and exercise her weak leg while she imagined herself walking and some-day running.

What hurt the most was that the local school wouldn't allow her to attend because she couldn't walk. She could hop a short distance on her good leg, but then her leg would get tired, and she would have to rest until she was able to hop some more.

She continued to work so hard at her leg exercises that the doctors eventually felt she was ready to be fitted with a heavy steel brace that supported her leg.

Now she could finally go to school, but school wasn't the happy place she had imagined. She felt lonely and left out as she watched the other children on the playground doing all the things she couldn't do. Some of her class-mates even made fun of her leg brace.

She continued to exercise her weak leg, and her family con-tinued to cheer her on in all her efforts. By age twelve, she was able to take the leg brace off for good.

In high school she became a star of her basketball and track teams, and her speed and agility attracted the attention of Ed Temple, the track coach at Tennessee State University (TSU).

In 1956 he invited her to attend his summer track program at TSU and train with the other track athletes there. She learned how to get off to a great start and how to move her arms and legs, as well as special exercises that made her stronger and faster.

She was soon traveling to races around the country. In 1956 she earned a spot on the US Olympic team, its youngest member.

At the 1956 Olympics in Melbourne, Australia, she did not do well in the 200-meter event, but she and her team won a bronze medal in the 400-meter relay.

As a woman:

After finishing her last two years of high school, she was awarded a track scholarship at Tennessee State University. She was the first member of her family to go to college.

She worked hard and, remembering what it felt like to stand on the winner's platform at the 1956 Olympics, she wanted another chance at winning an Olympic gold medal.

By 1960 she was faster than ever and made the Olympic team again. At the 1960 Olympics in Rome she was pitted against the greatest woman runner of that time, a German girl named Jutta Heine. Nobody had ever beaten Jutta, but in the 100-meter event, Wilma not only beat her and won her first gold medal, she won the event in eleven seconds flat and set a new world record. This was only eight-tenths of a second slower than the men's time.

She won again in the 200-meter event and again set a new world record. She now had two gold medals.

On the final day of the competition, she anchored the women's 400-meter relay, completing her sprinting reign by winning the event and again setting a new world record.

Her team won the relay in spite of the fact that, in her excitement, she almost dropped the baton and then had to make up the lost distance against Jutta Heine, which everyone believed was an impossible feat. But she did it and walked away from the 1960 Olympics with three gold medals.

She had achieved the impossible by becoming the first American woman to win three gold medals at a single Olympics.

After the 1960 Olympics, she was considered a hero to people all over the world, and she and her family were invited to the White House to meet President John F. Kennedy.

She was named United Press Athlete of the Year (1960), Associated Press Woman Athlete of the Year (1960, 1961), and became the first woman to receive the James E. Sullivan Award for Good Sportsmanship (1961).

After finishing college in 1963, she served as a teacher, track coach, athletic consultant, and assistant director of athletics for the Mayor's Youth Foundation in Chicago.

She worked to teach sports to underprivileged youth, hoping that success in sports would keep them in school. In 1981 she set up her own foundation to nurture young athletes and teach them that they, too, could succeed despite all the odds against them.

Throughout her life, she spoke out for the things she cared about such as segregation and the value of athletics in building character and was always a role model and inspiration to others.

Through her dedication to her dream and her belief in herself, she overcame obstacles of illness and poverty and achieved the impossible. She not only walked, she *ran*!

Once known as the sickliest child in her hometown, she had become the fastest woman in the world. She had dreamed big and worked hard, and she was a winner in sports and in life.

"I can't are two words that have never been in my vocabulary."
—Wilma Rudolph (1940–1994)

Arthur **Ashe**

They chased him off the tennis court.

AP Photo

As a boy:

Arthur was born in 1943 and, as a black child growing up in segregated Richmond, Virginia, no one would have ever predicted that one day he would be a world-class athlete.

He was "skinny as a soda straw," and he spent much of his time reading and listening to music with his mother Mattie.

When he was four, his family moved to a five-room frame house in the middle of Brook Field Park, a blacks-only park that stretched over eighteen acres.

It was always the tennis courts that were the star attraction for him, and in spite of his small size, he learned to swing a tennis racket fast and hard.

He learned the love of books and reading from his mother and the importance of self-discipline and hard work from his father, who worked several jobs to support the family. His dad also taught him to "always be a gentleman" and that "the way you played the game was what was important—not who won."

As his world expanded, he was drawn to the sixteen tennis courts at Byrd Park, a whites-only tennis complex where he could watch but not play. He stood behind the fence watching until someone shouted at him to go back to his "own part of town."

That's when he really began to understand what being black meant: not being allowed to play in the parks for white people, having to ride in the back of a bus even when there was a seat in the front, having to live in "the other part of town," and having to go to "those other schools."

Back at Brook Field, things were a lot better. That was his domain, and it did not take him long to get to know Ronald Charity, a college student who taught tennis at Brook Field during the summers. Charity was the best black tennis player in Richmond, and when Arthur was seven, Charity offered to help him. That was the beginning of Arthur's serious tennis instruction.

Then more help arrived when Arthur was ten. Charity asked Dr. Robert W. Johnson to help Arthur, and for eight consecutive summers, Arthur headed to Johnson's summer tennis camp. At Johnson's camp, not only were practice and drill emphasized, but so was the importance of good manners and composure on the court. He was told that there is "no excuse for poor manners."

As he grew taller, his game improved even more, now that he could race from line to line as well as extend his racket to snag balls his opponents thought were winners.

In 1955 he won the singles championship in the American Tennis Association's twelve-and-under competition, but he was not allowed to enter a Richmond match sponsored by the Middle Atlantic chapter of the US Lawn Tennis Association because he was black.

The rejection was a bitter blow, but even though he was banned from some local tennis courts and tournaments because of the color of his skin, he always kept his cool. In moments of humiliation he learned to walk away with what was left of his dignity rather than lose it all in an explosion of rage.

As a man:

Upon graduation from high school, he earned a tennis scholarship to the University of California at Los Angeles (UCLA), the first black student to be given a scholarship there. At UCLA he put in 250 hours of work a year, and it wasn't long before he became recognized for his tennis ability on a national level.

In 1963 he became the first African American male to play on the courts at Wimbledon and the first African American to make the US Davis Cup team.

In 1964 he was the winner of the Johnston Award, one of our country's most prestigious tennis honors awarded annually to the American tennis player who contributes the most to the growth of the sport while exhibiting good sportsmanship and character.

By 1965 he was ranked third in our country and sixth in the world in the amateur tennis rankings.

In August 1968 he won both the United States National and the United States Open singles titles and became the top-ranked amateur tennis player in the United States.

By 1974 people were wondering if he was spending too much time on his social causes and not enough on his game since he had not won a major singles event since 1970 when he captured the Australian Open. But in 1975, again rising to the challenge, he had one of his greatest seasons ever—winning Wimbledon and once again attaining the ultimate ranking of number one in the world.

He retired from competitive tennis in 1980 following heart surgery and was named captain of the US Davis Cup team in 1981.

He was inducted into the Tennis Hall of Fame in 1985, and in 1992 he was named "Sports Illustrated Sportsman of the Year."

In 1991 he went public with the news that he had AIDS, which he had contracted from a blood transfusion during his heart surgery. By going public, he helped the country begin to look at AIDS victims with more compassion and less fear.

He was a trailblazer for African American men in tennis in much the say way Althea Gibson had been for African American women some ten years earlier.

His accomplishments in the tennis world are all the more remarkable when one remembers that tennis was looked on as a gentleman's sport, a game played by rich white boys, not by poor black boys.

For Arthur, tennis was always about much more than personal glory and awards. His position as a world-class athlete gave him the opportunity to speak out about inequities, both in the tennis world and in society as a whole. He used this opportunity to bring about humanitarian change whenever possible. That is what makes his legacy so unique and so important.

He was born in a blacks-only hospital, grew up in blacks-only neighborhoods, and went to blacks-only schools, yet he rose and triumphed in a sport dominated by whites because he refused to let the color of his skin limit the scope of his dreams.

"I want no stain on my character, no blemish on my reputation."
—Arthur Ashe (1943–1993)

Ben **Carson**

The boy with the knife.

AP Photo/Gail Burton

As a boy:

Ben was born in Detroit, Michigan, in 1951, and he and his brother were raised by their mother, who often worked two or three jobs to support the family.

As a young boy, he didn't like to read books, and he was always at the bottom of his class. He still remembers how in the fifth grade he was failing almost every subject, but he remembers one incident in particular.

His class had just taken a math quiz, and it was the custom for the students to report their math scores out loud, so the teacher could record the scores in her book.

When he got his quiz back from the girl behind him who had corrected it, he had gotten zero out of thirty right.

89

He tried to mumble "none," hoping the teacher would mis-understand him, and she did. She thought he had said "nine," and she raved about how wonderful that was until the girl behind him couldn't stand it any longer, and she corrected the teacher.

Everybody roared with laughter, and Ben was so humiliated that he just wanted to evaporate into thin air and disappear forever.

It was about this time when he heard about mission doc-tors who helped people in far-off lands, but his mother reminded him that he could never be a doctor if he didn't start reading books and stop watching so much TV.

From then on, every time he reached for the TV, his mother told him to read a book instead. She also insisted that he and his broth-er write book reports for the books they read. They didn't know at the time that she couldn't read their reports because of her third-grade education. The more he read, the more interesting books became, and before long he was devouring them. Within two years he rose from the bottom of his class to the top.

But his problems weren't over yet. He also had a patholog-ical temper, which scared his family. He remembers once when he tried to hit his mother in the head with a hammer because he didn't want to wear something she wanted him to wear.

He also put a three-inch gash in a classmate's forehead with his lock when he tried to close Ben's locker.

And then at fourteen, he stabbed a friend in the abdomen with a large camping knife when his friend tried to change the radio station they were listening to. Fortunately, the knife hit his friend's belt buckle, which saved his life, but this shook Ben up so badly that he went home, locked himself in the bathroom, and did some serious thinking.

He knew that in spite of the good grades he was now earn-ing, he could end up in jail, reform school, or the grave because of his temper and never be the doctor he wanted to be.

He spent three hours in the bathroom praying about his temper and reading the book of Proverbs. When he came out of the bathroom, his temper was gone. He had concluded during his stint in the bathroom that if people can make you angry, they can control you, and he refused to give that control to anyone else.

As a man:

During his last year of high school, he had to choose a college, but each college application cost ten dollars. He had only a single ten-dollar bill, which meant he could apply to only one school, so he chose Yale University after watching the Yale team beat Harvard on his favorite TV quiz show, *College Bowl.*

Fortunately, he was accepted by Yale and received an academic scholarship that covered most of his college expenses.

He worked hard at Yale and read even more than his teachers assigned. After Yale, he attended the Michigan Medical School, where he discovered his surgical skills. Again, he would put a knife in his hand, but this time to save lives, not to take them.

During his hospital training, he discovered his love of neurosurgery, which, along with his natural ability, would soon take him to the top of his field.

When he was ready to begin his internship, he applied to Johns Hopkins Hospital, which received over 125 applications to join its neurosurgery division each year, and it accepted only two. These odds did not scare him off because he recalled his mother's words that he could become whatever he wanted to be.

He was accepted at Johns Hopkins and always treated everyone with equal respect, whether an orderly or another doctor. He also learned to deal with racism again when some of the nurses would assume he was an orderly because he was black or when some of the patients would not allow him to touch them because he was black.

He completed his two-year internship in just one year and then completed his four-year residency there.

At age thirty-three he became the director of pediatric neurosurgery at Johns Hopkins, the youngest chief of pediatric neurosurgery in US history, and he began to see some very important cases.

One of these cases was a four-year-old girl with a severe form of epilepsy that sometimes caused her to have as many as a hundred seizures a day. Ben and his medical team performed a dangerous operation where they removed part of the left side of her brain (hemispherectomy). If the surgery were successful, she would be free of her seizures. But if the surgery failed, she could die. The surgery was successful, and now the whole medical world was watching him to see what he would no next.

He was also the primary surgeon in the dramatic and successful twenty-two-hour operation in 1987 that separated the West German Siamese twins who were joined at the back of the head.

He has not only attained his personal dream of being a doctor, but he has crossed color lines in his work, he has struggled against racial prejudice, and he has dealt with his own personal demons of anger and insecurity.

Children are very important to him, and he spends time speaking to schools and community centers—encouraging young people to work hard and believe in themselves and not let others set the limits for them.

"By THINKING BIG, we can transform our world."
                                    —Benjamin Carson, MD (1951–   )

Gloria Estefan

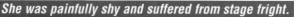

As a girl:

She was born Gloria Maria Fajardo on September 1, 1958, in Havana, Cuba, where her father was a motorcycle policeman assigned to the escort detail for President Fulgencio Batista and his family.

When Fidel Castro overthrew the Batista government in 1959, Cuba was no longer safe for Gloria and her family, so they fled to the United States for refuge.

After settling his family along with other Cuban refugees in Miami, her father returned to Cuba to fight against Fidel Castro.

Life was very difficult for the Cuban refugees in Miami because there were social problems as well as money problems. Many Americans didn't want so many Cuban refugees in their country, and they treated the refugees badly.

But Gloria was determined to succeed and worked very hard, always managing to be at the head of her class. And when things got tough, her mother and grandmother taught her to turn to music.

After serving in Cuba, Gloria's father returned to Miami, where he enlisted in the US Army and served in Vietnam for two years. When Gloria was ten, he returned home from Vietnam a very sick man. He was diagnosed with multiple sclerosis, and in just a few months he was no longer able to walk.

While her mother worked during the day and took classes at night to become a teacher, Gloria for the next six years became a little mother to her family. She took care of both her younger sister Rebecca and her ailing father.

This was a very difficult time for her, and when the burden of caring for her family sometimes became too much for her, she would find temporary escape by locking herself in her room and playing her guitar. She found she was able to forget her problems for a while as she sang along with the ballads and pop songs she loved. Instead of crying, she expressed her pain through music.

During her teen years she was quiet, shy, and a "little chubby." Her music became more important than ever to her as her father's condition worsened, and when she was sixteen, he had to be moved to a Veterans Administration hospital.

During her senior year of high school she and some girlfriends put together a band, and the father of one of the band members invited Emilio Estefan, a popular band leader in Miami, to listen to the girls and give them some tips.

She met Emilio again a few months later when she attended a wedding where he and his band, the Miami Latin Boys, were playing. He asked her to sing a song with his band, and a few weeks later he asked her to join his band permanently.

He agreed to let her perform only on weekends and vacations, so that she could finish college at the University of Miami.

After Gloria joined Emilio's band, it developed a different, very special sound, and Emilio changed the band's name from the Miami Latin Boys to the Miami Sound Machine.

Being painfully shy, the most difficult part of being in the band for her was overcoming her stage fright.

As a woman:

Gloria and Emilio became very close and were married in 1978, three months after she graduated from college.

The same year the Miami Sound Machine released its first album, *Renacer (Live Again)*, and during the next two years it released two more albums that sold well in Miami but didn't get much attention anywhere else.

In 1980 there was bad news and good news: Gloria's father died, but her son Nayib was born.

During the next several years the Miami Sound Machine released four Spanish-language albums, and from those albums came a dozen songs that became worldwide hits.

Throughout the rest of the 1980s, Gloria and the band not only continued to record Spanish-language songs but also began to record more and more English-language songs. Then in 1984 their first English-language single, "Dr. Beat," became a hit.

Their next two albums, *Eyes of Innocence* (1984) and *Primitive Love* (1985), made Gloria and the Miami Sound Machine a success all over English-speaking America.

On March 19, 1990, President George H. W. Bush honored Gloria for her drug prevention work with teenagers. But the next day tragedy struck when her tour bus was in an accident during a snowstorm on the way to the band's next concert in New York.

Her back was broken in the accident, and she thought her career might be over. She underwent a new and very risky kind of surgery that, if not successful, could leave her paralyzed forever. The operation was successful and, after many months of extensive physical therapy and determination on her part, she was performing again.

Gloria is not only passionate about her music, but she is also a passionate and tireless worker for those with problems. People throughout Miami call her "a star with a heart."

When Hurricane Andrew roared through Miami in 1992, she and Emilio organized a benefit concert that raised millions of dollars for the hurricane victims. And she has also worked hard for many years to help battered and abused children in Miami.

After her back surgery, she wasn't sure she would be able to have any more children, but in 1994 Gloria and Emilio became proud parents again with the birth of their daughter Emily.

Even though she is considered a superstar in the world of music, she is most proud of the Ellis Island Congressional Medal of Honor she received in 1993 (the highest award the United States gives to a citizen born outside the country) for being a positive representative of Cuban immigrants as well as a worldwide ambassador for the United States.

Through her music, she has shattered cultural and gender lines across the globe and has been a successful wife, mother, singer, songwriter, diplomat, movie star, and humanitarian.

"In my music I like to focus on things that bring us together, not things that tear us apart."

—Gloria Estefan (1957–   )

Ellen **Ochoa**

Photo courtesy of NASA

As a girl:

Ellen was born in 1958 in Los Angeles, California, and grew up in the town of La Mesa, a suburb of San Diego. She is half Mexican and is proud of her Hispanic heritage.

Her grandparents were born in Mexico but moved to the United States to raise their family because they wanted their children to have as many educational advantages and opportunities as possible.

Ellen's mother was a firm believer in the value of education and taught her five children that if they worked hard and got a good education, they could be anything they wanted to be.

97

She was also a good role model for her children because she practiced what she preached. She took college classes for twenty-three years while rearing her family and eventually earned her degree, taking one class at a time. She was always talking about her classes and passed her enthusiasm for education on to all her children.

Ellen loved school and was not afraid to work hard. Her favorite subjects were math and music, but she did well in all of her classes.

She also loved to read, and one of her favorite books was *A Wrinkle in Time* because it was a story about a young girl who traveled through time.

Neil Armstrong first walked on the moon when Ellen was eleven years old, and it never occurred to her that she, too, might someday become an astronaut.

She loved school, and she loved academic challenges. When she was thirteen, she won the San Diego spelling bee, and she was also named "outstanding seventh- and eighth-grade student."

Even though her father left the family when she was in junior high, her mother continued to encourage her children to work hard in school and set high goals for themselves.

Ellen learned to play the flute, and music was the common bond among her and her siblings. She and her brothers and sister were all in either the marching band, the orchestra, or the choir in junior high and high school.

She became such an accomplished musician that she played with the Civic Youth Orchestra in San Diego while in high school. She even thought that one day she might have a career as a classical flutist.

While in high school, she continued to be an exceptional student and graduated as the valedictorian of her high school class in 1975.

At that time, girls were not encouraged to take the "hard math and science courses." In spite of the fact that she was the top math student in her high school, no one told her how a person, especially a woman, could get a job in the mathematics field.

And even though girls weren't encouraged to go to college and major in math and science, her high school calculus teacher made math so appealing and exciting that she decided to continue studying it in college.

As a woman:

At San Diego State University, she changed her major five times before finally choosing physics (music, business administration, journalism, computer science, then physics).

Physics proved to be a good choice. She was again the valedictorian of her graduating class and went on to earn her master of science degree and doctorate in electrical engineering at Stanford University.

While in graduate school, some of her friends applied to be astronauts at the National Aeronautics and Space Administration (NASA), which was now open to women as well as men. After learning that she would be eligible to apply as soon as she finished her degree, she decided that she, too, would apply for the astronaut corps.

After leaving school, she made her mark first as a researcher developing and patenting optical techniques for use in space and industry and then at NASA's Ames Research Center where she became chief of the intelligent systems technology branch.

In 1990 she took the next step toward fulfilling her ambition to become an astronaut by surviving a selection process that began with thousands of applicants. She then completed a year of intensive training before qualifying in July 1991 when she became the first female Hispanic astronaut.

In April 1993 she was the only woman on a crew of five astronauts aboard the shuttle *Discovery* when it was launched into space. She made history as the first Hispanic woman astronaut ever to travel in outer space.

She orbited the earth for nine days in the *Discovery* shuttle, supervising research into the chemical composition of the upper atmosphere, ozone layer depletion, and changes in the sun's radiation level.

In November 1994 she made a second trip into space aboard the space shuttle *Atlantis*. During this eleven-day flight she conducted more solar studies, focusing on the sun's energy and the effect it has on the earth's atmosphere.

Astronauts are allowed to take two personal items with them on their space flights, and she chose to take her flute and a picture of her husband.

Since her *Atlantis* mission, she has completed her third and fourth space missions and continued to work for NASA on robotics and space station research and development. Some day she would like to go back into space again, possibly living on a space station or maybe even joining a journey to Mars.

She now jokes that her gender was more of a problem for her than her Hispanic heritage as far as her technical educational pursuits because her advisers tended to steer her away from the "hard" math and engineering courses.

She enjoys talking to students, especially Hispanic students, about the need to study and work hard to achieve life's goals.

"Don't be afraid to reach for the stars."
—Ellen Ochoa (1958–   )

Michael **Jordan**

He was suspended from high school.

AP Photo/Kathy Willens

As a boy:

Michael was born in Brooklyn, New York, in 1963. Soon after his birth, his family moved to North Carolina, where he grew up loving sports and loving a challenge.

His father became a supervisor at a General Electric plant, his mother became head of customer relations at a bank, and both parents taught their children the value of hard work.

Baseball was Michael's first love, and he pitched two no-hitters in Little League. Then he graduated to the Babe Ruth League and received the Most Valuable Player (MVP) award when his team won the state championship.

Dare to Dream!

By the time he got to junior high, he was playing football, basketball, and baseball and was a good all-around athlete.

In addition to his natural ability, there were two things that helped him become a great athlete. He hated losing and he loved a challenge, so he always worked very hard. The greater the challenge, the harder he worked.

He also had a great deal of support from his parents, who came to all his games and always found a way to praise him, no matter which team won.

When he got to high school, he was still playing three sports and was starting point guard with the junior varsity basketball squad. He was hoping to get picked for the varsity team at the end of the season, but the coach picked a taller player instead. The only way he could go to the state championship tournament was as a substitute manager, so he watched the game from the bench while handing out towels. When the season ended, he vowed that he would make the varsity team next season no matter how much work it took.

He began working harder than ever on his basketball skills and even started cutting classes to spend more time in the gym practicing. He didn't take his teachers' warnings seriously and finally ended up being suspended for cutting class.

After his suspension, his father told him he would never get to college if he kept cutting classes, so he cut no more classes.

He kept on practicing basketball, and in the summer before his junior year, he grew a full five inches. Now he was six feet three inches tall, and his father said later, "It was almost as if Michael willed himself taller."

He had already given up football to get ready for the basketball season, and after his junior year, he stopped playing baseball, too. Then it was just basketball and more basketball!

He had double practice sessions every day, practicing with the junior varsity team from 5:30 PM to 7 PM and then staying to practice with the varsity from 7 PM to 9 PM.

As a high school senior, he was almost six feet five inches tall and worked as hard as ever, averaging 27.8 points and 12 rebounds per game. He was averaging nearly a point a minute, and fans were now flocking to see him.

After he stopped cutting classes for basketball, he became a good student and graduated from high school in June of 1981.

As a man:

After graduating from high school, Michael enrolled at the University of North Carolina at Chapel Hill, where he not only made the basketball team (the Tar Heels) but also the starting lineup.

Photos of his last-second shot that won the national championship for the Tar Heels appeared in magazines and newspapers across the country.

He wound up scoring 16 points in the final game, and his average for his freshman season was 13.5 points a game, which helped his team to a great 32–2 record.

He continued to work as hard as ever on the basketball court, trying to be the best player he could possibly be. He was at his best at "crunch time," the last few minutes of a close game.

He was named College Basketball's Player of the Year the following two seasons, the highest honor a player can receive.

Then at the end of his junior year, he had a difficult decision to make: whether to come back for his last year of college or turn pro. He finally decided to take advantage of the opportunity to move up to a higher level, so on May 5, 1984, he announced he would turn pro.

In June of 1984 he was drafted by the Chicago Bulls, but before joining the Bulls in Chicago, his dream of competing in the Olympics was realized when he was named cocaptain of the 1984 US Olympic basketball team. Past US teams had dominated Olympic basketball, and the United States won a gold medal again in 1984.

When he returned from the Olympics, the Chicago Bulls welcomed him home, hoping he would help the team improve its record. In the two years before the team drafted Michael, it had records of 28–54 and 27–55 and had not made the playoffs either year. But Michael just saw this as another challenge.

He played well right from the beginning, using his speed to blow past veteran players and using his jumping ability to soar over them. He was scoring from every spot on the court and sometimes stayed up in the air so long he seemed to defy gravity.

He found the pro game was much harder than college basketball. The players were bigger, stronger, quicker, and better, but this just challenged him to work even harder.

In 1985 at the end of his first season as a pro, both the *Sporting News* and the NBA named him "Rookie of the Year."

By this time he was becoming one of the most popular athletes in the country, but he still found time to visit sick children in hospitals and work with the Special Olympics and the "Just Say No to Drugs" program as well as other charities in the Chicago area.

He was named the NBA's Most Valuable Player (MVP) five times, led the Chicago Bulls to six NBA championships, and won his second gold medal as a member of the 1992 US Olympic basketball "Dream Team."

As one of America's best-loved sports heroes, there has never been an athlete quite like him and there may never be again.

"I learned the value of hard work and persistence from my family."
—Michael Jordan (1963–   )

Sammy **Sosa**

He dropped out of school to help provide for his family.

As a boy:

The boy we all know today as "Sluggin' Sammy" was born in the Dominican Republic in 1968, the fifth of seven children.

His family lived in a one-bedroom house with dirt floors and no indoor plumbing, but the family was very close and there was a lot of love. He learned a strong work ethic from his father and a deep sense of honesty from his mother.

When Sammy was six, his father died, and now everyone in the family had to work. His mother cooked and washed clothes for people while Sammy and his brothers and sisters washed cars, sold fruit on the street, and shined shoes.

But even with everyone in the family working, times were very hard, and sometimes there was only enough food for one meal a day.

Baseball was the most popular sport in the Dominican Republic, and Sammy and the kids in his neighborhood made their own baseball equipment from cardboard boxes and burlap bags. His first glove was actually made from an inside-out milk carton.

They made their rough bats from branches of vasima trees, and they even made their own balls by wrapping old golf balls they found with torn nylon stockings their mothers had thrown away. Then they wrapped the stocking-covered golf balls with black tape.

The difference between eating and not eating often depended upon which shoeshine boy reached a tourist first, and many times the kids who shined shoes had to literally fight for their customers.

One day twelve-year-old Sammy was the first shoeshine boy to reach a tourist named Bill Chase. This tourist was a US citizen who owned a local shoe factory, and he was so impressed by Sammy's strong work ethic and determination that eventually he hired Sammy and his brothers to sweep floors and clean the machinery at his factory.

When Sammy was thirteen, Bill Chase bought him his first real baseball glove, and Sammy and his family were treated like part of Bill's own family.

Even though Sammy loved school, he decided to drop out in the eighth grade so that he could work full time to help provide for his family. And with the extra money coming in from working full time at the factory, he could spend more time playing baseball.

Over the next few years people began to recognize the talents of this tall, thin outfielder with a wild but powerful swing. When he was fifteen, the Philadelphia Phillies offered him a contract to play in the States on one of its farm teams. Sammy signed immediately because of his love for baseball but also because he knew if he had a successful career in baseball, he could help his family escape their life of poverty.

That contract was canceled because baseball officials in the United States felt Sammy was too young, but a year later the Texas Rangers offered him a professional contract.

He had been given another chance to pursue his dream of a professional baseball career.

As a man:

When seventeen-year-old Sammy arrived in the United States in 1986, he had already worked very hard for ten years, helping to support his family any way he could. But now he faced new challenges: the problem of racism and the danger of drugs.

He managed to avoid both those problems, but he still found his move to the United States very difficult because he missed his close-knit family and because he knew very little English.

In his first few years in professional baseball, he had to work as hard on his fielding as on his hitting, but he was used to hard work and he never gave up or stopped trying.

In 1989 he was traded to the Chicago White Sox. In August 1989 he played his first game for the White Sox against the Minnesota Twins, going three-for-three with a home run and two RBI.

But Sammy was still struggling at the plate, and in 1992 he was traded again. This time he was traded to the Chicago Cubs, where he began working with the Cubs' batting coach, Billy Williams, and his performance at the plate began to improve.

With new confidence in his hitting, he started the 1993 season strong, and he just kept improving. He hit more home runs, drove in more runs, and had a higher batting average in 1993 than he had ever had in a full season.

One of the highlights of his 1993 season was joining the "30–30 club"—a nickname given to the few players who have stolen thirty or more bases and hit thirty or more home runs in a single season.

A wrist injury in 1996 disabled him for part of the season, but in 1997 he came back stronger than ever. He recorded the one thousandth base hit and two hundredth home run of his career.

Sammy led the Cubs to the playoffs in 1998 and was voted the National League's Most Valuable Player (MVP). In 1999 he became the first player in baseball history to hit sixty home runs in back-to-back seasons, and in 2001 he became the first player in history to surpass sixty home runs three times.

In spite of his successful baseball career, he has never forgotten the people of the Dominican Republic. He arranged for hundreds of computers to be donated to Dominican schools, and he even established his own baseball academy with playing fields and dormitories. He wanted the kids back home to have the facilities and teachers to learn the game of baseball that he never had.

In 1998 he created the Sammy Sosa Foundation, an organization that raises funds for underprivileged children both in the Chicago area and in the Dominican Republic. He was also honored as one of the recipients of the Gene Autry Courage Award—an award given to an athlete who has demonstrated heroism in the face of difficulty or adversity, overcoming hardships to inspire others.

He rose from poverty to become one of our most celebrated sports heroes and is truly a credit to the game of baseball.

As Sammy has often said in his interviews, "Baseball has been very good to me." But Sammy has also been very good to baseball.

"My life is a celebration of faith."

—Sammy Sosa (1968–   )

Heather **Whitestone**

AP Photo/Tom Costello

As a girl:

Heather was born a perfectly healthy baby in Alabama in 1973, but when she was eighteen months old, she developed a dangerously high fever that left her profoundly deaf.

Doctors predicted that she would never develop much verbal speech, would probably not develop beyond a third-grade educational level, and recommended that some sort of vocational training be considered for her.

The massive infection had also left her body so weak that she had to learn to walk all over again.

As a young girl, her deafness was an ever-present source

of frustration. When her sisters were outside playing, she was usually inside practicing speech exercises. And she always felt like an outsider at school because when the other kids laughed and talked about things, she had no idea what they were laughing and talking about.

She didn't like feeling different from the other kids and worked hard just to keep up with them. Schoolwork was difficult for her. She was a slow reader and found English grammar very difficult.

The one place where she found refuge from her feelings of being an "outsider" was in the dance studio. There she could communicate with body language, and words weren't necessary.

Ballet taught her patience and a respect for the learning process. Soon dancing began to fill her dreams, and she imagined herself twirling onstage in the spotlight free from all of the frustrations of life and learning.

There were also her daydreams where she would stand in front of the bathroom mirror with a headband on her head, pretending to be Miss America.

Her parents did not allow her to sign at home because they wanted her to learn to talk so that she would grow up being part of the hearing world.

When she was twelve, she asked to go to a school for the deaf, so she was enrolled at the Central Institute for the Deaf (CID) in St. Louis, Missouri. At her new school, both independence and good scholarship were encouraged.

She graduated from the CID at fourteen and believed that her years there provided both the academic and the social skills she would need to fulfill her dream of becoming a ballerina.

Back home at her public high school, few people took the time to try to communicate with her, and the dance studio once again became her safe haven.

After a year at the Alabama School of Fine Arts, she again returned to a public high school and began to dance with a group at the Briarwood Presbyterian Church.

She was as lonely as ever at high school. During her senior year, she decided to enter the County Junior Miss pageant because she wanted to be remembered by her class as someone other than just "the deaf girl."

As a woman:

During the pageant she spent a lot of time helping some of the other contestants with their choreography, which was a positive experience for everyone. She enjoyed helping them, and they were surprised to find out how easy it was to communicate with her.

On the final night of the pageant, when it was announced that she had won the "Spirit Award"—a scholarship awarded by the contestants themselves—she felt as if she'd just been voted homecoming queen of a dozen high schools.

She now realized that pageants were a way to make friends and earn scholarship money. It was time for college, and she chose Jacksonville State University in Jacksonville, Alabama, for two reasons: it had a special program to mainstream deaf students into regular classes and, just as important, four JSU students had won the Miss Alabama title.

As she watched the 1991 Miss America pageant at home with her mother, she was more sure than ever that she was on the right path to her dream of dancing ballet on the stage in Atlantic City.

Miss Hawaii was the first Miss Hawaii to ever win the crown. And those words—*the first*—sparked Heather's imagination. She knew that she wanted to dance ballet on that same Miss America stage in front of millions of television viewers.

111

When she won the Miss JSU title in 1992, she received a standing ovation from the audience. Now she had not only officially begun her journey toward fulfilling her dream, but she also felt more comfortable on the college campus and no longer so much like an outsider.

Next came the Miss Alabama pageant, where she was the first runner-up two years in a row.

Then in 1995 (her third try), she won the Miss Alabama title and went on to compete for the Miss America title.

When she was crowned Miss America in 1995, she became the first Miss America with a disability in the history of the pageant, and she inspired a nation.

In spite of being profoundly deaf, she had tried to live a normal life and had refused to listen to the voices of discouragement around her.

She had ignored the doctors who had predicted that she wouldn't develop beyond a third-grade educational level. She had ignored those who said she would never dance ballet. And she had ignored those who said she would never speak.

Since relinquishing her title, she has traveled the country, inspiring her audiences to overcome their own obstacles through what she calls her five-point STARS program (Success Through Action and Realization of your dreamS) consisting of a positive attitude, a belief in a dream, the willingness to work hard, to face your obstacles, and to build and use a strong support team.

Through her personal strength and unwavering dedication, she has proven that it is possible to make your dreams come true.

"Listen to your own heart and follow your own dream."
—Heather Whitestone (1973–   )

a final **thought**

Now that you have read these biographical sketches, you have probably begun to realize that people are much the same everywhere.

Regardless of the century in which they live or the area of the world, they all have pretty much the same kinds of problems, the same fears, the some hopes, and the same dreams.

All of us are given our own unique abilities and talents, but it is up to us to develop them and make the most of them.

All of us have obstacles to overcome. Some may come from outside ourselves and some may come from inside ourselves, but the attitude with which we meet these obstacles can mean the difference between failure and success, between defeat and victory.

Remember that your success is not necessarily measured by the world's standard of success but by the standard you set for yourself. You don't have to compete with anyone else to be successful. You just have to be the very best *you* that you can be.

If you did not find yourself in these pages, perhaps it is because you have your own dream. Whether your dream is small or large doesn't matter. But remember that you can never go any higher than your dream, so accept the challenge and have a dream.

Dare to Dream!

bibliography

Aaseng, Nathan. *Sports Great Michael Jordan*. Hillside, NJ: Enslow Publishers, 1992.

Adler, David A. *Jackie Robinson: He Was the First*. New York: Holiday House, 1989.

———. *Martin Luther King, Jr.: Free at Last*. New York: Holiday House, 1986.

Ashe, Arthur, and Arnold Rampersad. *Days of Grace: A Memoir*. New York: Alfred A. Knopf, 1993.

Benson, Michael. *Gloria Estefan*. Minneapolis: Lerner Publications, 2000.

Bolden, Tonya. *And Not Afraid to Dare: The Stories of Ten African-American Women*. New York: Scholastic Press, 1998.

Boulais, Sue. *Goria Estefan*. Childs, MD: Mitchell Lane, 1998.

Bracken, Thomas. *Abraham Lincoln*. Philadelphia: Chelsea House, 1998.

Brian, Denis. *Einstein: A Life*. New York: John Wiley & Sons, 1996.

Bruns, Roger A. *Abraham Lincoln*. New York: Chelsea House, 1986.

Buranelli, Vincent. *Thomas Alva Edison*. Englewoods Cliffs, NJ: Silver Burdett Press, 1989.

Carson, Benjamin S., MD. "Benjamin S. Carson, M.D." Hall of Science & Exploration Interview, June 29, 1996, Sun Valley, Idaho.

———. "Standing on God's Promise." *Guideposts* (June 1988).

115

Bibliography

Carson, Ben, MD, with Cecil Murphey. *Think Big*. Grand Rapids, MI: Zondervan, 1992.

Cary, Barbara. *Meet Abraham Lincoln*. New York: Random House, 2001.

Christensen, Bonnie. *The Daring Nellie Bly: America's Star Reporter*. New York: Alfred A. Knopf, 2003.

Coffey, Wayne. *Jim Thorpe*. Woodbridge, CT: Blackbirch Press, 1993.

Collins, David R. *Arthur Ashe: Against the Wind*. New York: Dillon Press, 1994.

Cosby, Bill. *Time Flies*. New York: Doubleday, 1987.

Darby, Jean. *Martin Luther King, Jr*. Minneapolis: Lerner Publications, 1990.

Detrich, Richard Lewis. *Norman Vincent Peale*. Milwaukee, WI: Ideals Publishing, 1979.

Edelman, Marian Wright. *Lanterns: A Memoir of Mentors*. Boston: Beacon Press, 1999.

———. *The Measure of Our Success: A Letter to My Children and Yours*. Boston: Beacon Press, 1994.

Faber, Doris, and Harold Faber. *Martin Luther King, Jr*. New York: Julian Messner, 1986.

Farris, Christine King. *My Brother Martin: A Sister Remembers*. New York: Simon & Schuster Books for Young Readers, 2003.

Fredeen, Charles. *Nellie Bly: Daredevil Reporter*. Minneapolis: Lerner Publications, 2000.

Gaines, Ann G. *Sammy Sosa*. Philadelphia: Chelsea House, 2000.

Gordon, Arthur. *Norman Vincent Peale: Minister to Millions*. Englewood Cliffs, NJ: Prentice-Hall, 1958.

Gray, Daphne, with Greg Lewis. *Yes, You Can Heather!* Grand Rapids, MI: Zondervan, 1995.

Greene, Carol. *Thomas Alva Edison: Bringer of Light*. Chicago: Children's Press, 1985.

Gutman, Bill. *Michael Jordan: Basketball Champ*. Brookfield, CT: Millbrook Press, 1992.

———. *Sammy Sosa: A Biography*. New York: Pocket Books, 1998.

Hacker, Carlotta. *Women in Profile: Scientists*. New York: Crabtree Publishing, 1998.

Harper, Jedith E. *Maya Angelou*. Chanhassen, MN: Child's World, 1999.

Herda, D. J. *Sandra Day O'Connor: Independent Thinker*. Springfield, NJ: Enslow Publishers, 1995.

Holland, Gini. *Sandra Day O'Connor*. Austin, TX: Steck-Vaughn Company, 1997.

Houghton, Sarah. *Michael Jordan: The Best Ever*. Mankato, MN: Capstone Press, 2002.

Jakoubek, Robert. *Martin Luther King, Jr*. New York: Chelsea House, 1989.

Jones, Amy Robin. *Toni Morrison: Journey to Freedom*. Chanhassen, MN: Child's World, 2002.

Kendall, Martha E. *Nellie Bly: Reporter for the World*. Brookfield, CT: Millbrook Press, 1992.

King, David C. *First Facts about American Heroes*. New York: Blackbirch Press, 1996.

Kite, L. Patricia. *Maya Angelou*. Minneapolis: Lerner Publications, 1999.

Kramer, Barbara. *Toni Morrison: Nobel Prize–Winning Author*. Springfield, NJ: Enslow Publishers, 1996.

Krull, Kathleen. *Wilma Unlimited: How Wilma Rudolph Became the World's Fastest Woman*. New York: Harcourt Brace & Company, 1996.

Kudlinski, Kathleen V. *Helen Keller: A Light for the Blind*. New York: Viking Kestrel, 1989.

Laezman, Rick. *100 Hispanic-Americans Who Shaped American History*. San Mateo, CA: Bluewood Books, 2002.

Lampton, Christopher. *Thomas Alva Edison*. New York: Franklin Watts, 1988.

Lazo, Caroline. *Arthur Ashe*. Minneapolis: Lerner Publications, 1999.
———. *Martin Luther King, Jr*. New York: Dillon Press, 1994.

LeSourd, Leonard, Arthur Gordon, Van Varner, and Fulton Oursler Jr. "Norman Vincent Peale." *Guideposts* (April 1994).

Lipsyte, Robert. *Jim Thorpe: 20th Century Jock*. New York: HarperCollins, 1993.

117

Bibliography

Long, Barbara. *Jim Thorpe: Legendary Athlete*. Springfield: NJ: Enslow Publishers, 1997.

Lovitt, Chip. *Michael Jordan*. New York: Scholastic Press, 1993.

Lowery, Linda. *Martin Luther King Day*. Minneapolis: Carolrhoda Books, 1987.

Machamer, Gene. *Hispanic American Profiles*. New York: Ballantine Books, 1996.

Markham, Lois. *Helen Keller*. New York: Franklin Watts, 1993.

McCallum, Heather Whitestone. *Believing the Promise*. New York: Doubleday, 1999.

McGrayne, Sharon Bertsch. *Nobel Prize Women in Science*. New York: Carol Publishing Group, 1993.

Morey, Janet Nomura, and Wendy Dunn. *Famous Asian Americans*. New York: Cobblehill Books, 1992.

———. *Famous Hispanic Americans*. New York: Cobblehill Books, 1996.

Myers, Walter Dean. *Young Martin's Promise*. Austin, TX: Steck-Vaughn Company, 1993.

Nardo, Don. *The Importance of Jim Thorpe*. San Diego, CA: Lucent Books, 1994.

North, Sterling. *Abe Lincoln: Log Cabin to White House*. New York: Random House, 1984.

O'Connor, Sandra Day, and Alan H. Day. *Lazy B: Growing Up on a Cattle Ranch in the American Southwest*. New York: Random House, 2002.

Palacios, Argentina. *Standing Tall: The Stories of Ten Hispanic Americans*. New York: Scholastic Press, 1994.

Patrick-Wexler, Diane. *Toni Morrison*. Austin, TX: Steck-Vaughn Company, 1997.

Peale, Norman Vincent. *The True Joy of Positive Living: An Autobiography*. New York: William Morrow and Company, 1984.

Peters, Sarah Whitaker. *Becoming O'Keeffe*. New York: Abbeville Press, 1991.

Pettit, Jayne. *Maya Angelou: Journey of the Heart*. New York: Dutton/Lodestar Books, 1996.

Quackenbush, Robert. *Arthur Ashe and His Match with History*. New York: Simon & Schuster Books for Young Readers, 1994.

Reef, Catherine. *Albert Einstein*. Minneapolis: Dillon Press, 1991.

Richards, Gregory B. *Jim Thorpe: World's Greatest Athlete*. Chicago: Children's Press, 1984.

Robinson, Roxana. *Georgia O'Keeffe: A Life*. New York: Harper & Row, 1989.

Rodriguez, Janel. *Gloria Estefan*. Austin, TX: Steck-Vaughn Company, 1996.

Romero, Maritza. *Ellen Ochoa: The First Hispanic Woman Astronaut*. New York: Rosen Publishing Group's PowerKids Press, 1997.

Rosenberg, Robert. *Bill Cosby: The Changing Black Image*. Brookfield, CT: Millbrook Press, 1991.

Ruth, Amy. *Wilma Rudolph*. Minneapolis: Lerner Publications, 2000.

Sandburg, Carl. *Abe Lincoln Grows Up*. New York: Harcourt Brace Jovanovich, 1956.

Sanford, William R., and Carl R. Green. *Jackie Robinson*. New York: Crestwood House, 1992.

Scott, Richard. *Jackie Robinson*. New York: Chelsea House, 1987.

Severance, John B. *Einstein: Visionary Scientist*. New York: Clarion Books, 1999.

Sherrow, Victoria. *Wilma Rudolph*. Minneapolis: Carolrhoda Books, 2000.

Shuker, Nancy. *Maya Angelou*. Englewood Cliffs, NJ: Silver Burdett Press, 1990.

Siegel, Beatrice. *Marian Wright Edelman: The Making of a Crusader*. New York: Simon & Schuster Books for Young Readers, 1995.

Sills, Leslie. *Inspirations: Stories about Women Artists*. Niles, IL: Albert Whitman & Company, 1989.

Simmons, Alex. *Ben Carson*. Austin, TX: Steck-Vaughn Company, 1996.

Sinnott, Susan. *Extraordinary Asian Pacific Americans*. Chicago: Children's Press, 1993.

Smith, Kathie Billingslea. *Martin Luther King, Jr*. New York: Simon & Schuster, 1987.

119

Bibliography

Smith, Ronald L. *Cosby: The Life of a Comedy Legend*. Amherst, NY: Prometheus Books, 1997.

Sosa, Sammy. *Sosa: An Autobiography*. New York: Warner Books, 2000.

Spangenburg, Ray, and Diane K. Moser. *Eleanor Roosevelt: A Passion to Improve*. New York: Facts on File, 1997.

Sullivan, George. *Helen Keller*. New York: Scholastic Press, 2000.

Turner, Robyn. *Georgia O'Keeffe*. Boston: Little, Brown, and Company, 1991.

Venezia, Mike. *Georgia O'Keeffe*. Chicago: Children's Press, 1993.

Weidt, Maryann N. *Stateswoman to the World*. Minneapolis: Carolrhoda Books, 1991.

Wepman, Dennis. *Helen Keller*. New York: Chelsea House, 1987.

Whitestone, Heather, with Angela Elwell Hunt. *Listening with My Heart*. New York: Doubleday, 1997.

Winner, David. *Eleanor Roosevelt*. Milwaukee: Gareth Stevens Publishing, 1991.

acknowledgments

Every effort has been made to locate the copyright holders of all copyrighted material and to secure the necessary permissions to reproduce them. In the event of any questions arising as to their use, the publisher will be glad to make changes in future printings.

Photo credits: All photos courtesy of AP/Wide World with the following exceptions: p. 21, Carnegie Library of Pittsburgh [Bly]; p. 49, Library of Congress [Wu]; p. 77, Children's Defense Fund [Edelman]; p. 93, Sony Music [Estefan]; p. 97, NASA [Ochoa].